Potential Russia

Potential Russia

Richard Washburn Child

Edited and Introduction by
Lee A. Farrow

Anthem Press
An imprint of Wimbledon Publishing Company
www.anthempress.com

This edition first published in UK and USA 2025
by ANTHEM PRESS
75–76 Blackfriars Road, London SE1 8HA, UK
or PO Box 9779, London SW19 7ZG, UK
and
244 Madison Ave #116, New York, NY 10016, USA

© 2025 Richard Washburn Child

The author asserts the moral right to be identified as the author of this work.

All rights reserved. Without limiting the rights under copyright reserved above,
no part of this publication may be reproduced, stored or introduced into
a retrieval system, or transmitted, in any form or by any means
(electronic, mechanical, photocopying, recording or otherwise),
without the prior written permission of both the copyright
owner and the above publisher of this book.

British Library Cataloguing-in-Publication Data
A catalogue record for this book is available from the British Library.

Library of Congress Cataloging-in-Publication Data: 2024943701
A catalog record for this book has been requested.

ISBN-13: 978-1-83999-336-7 (Hbk)/ 978-1-83999-337-4 (Pbk)
ISBN-10: 1-83999-336-7 (Hbk)/ 1-83999-337-5 (Pbk)

Cover Credit: GetArchive LLC, public domain

This title is also available as an e-book.

CONTENTS

Introduction		1
1.	Between Yesterday and Tomorrow	11
2.	Cannon Meat	15
3.	All for Russia	21
4.	The Blight	29
5.	Czar and People	41
6.	Bureaucracy and National Spirit	49
7.	Russia's Better Half	59
8.	The Miracle Measure	75
9.	The Future of Russia	79
10.	Resources and Development	91
11.	A Call to America	99
Index		111

INTRODUCTION

In 1916, less than a year before the Russian Revolution, Richard Washburn Child rejected rumors of impending turmoil: "Cool heads in Russia believe the idea of revolution is ridiculous. Something less dramatic is in store for Russia." On the contrary, Child detected a new nationalism, a surge in a Russian spirit infused with religion and fealty to the Tsar, that existed not only among the peasants and the military but even among bureaucrats and workers. Despite the stresses of war, he believed, "There was not even the glimmer of revolution." Child wrote these words approximately a year before Tsar Nicholas II would abdicate the throne and Vladimir Lenin would return to Russia and lead the Bolsheviks in a seizure of power. Indeed, Child's prediction about the impossibility of a revolution or a separate peace was but one of many things that he got wrong in his appraisal of Russia. But it is precisely these miscalculations that make his book a fascinating read. Child believed that he understood Russia, but his failure to sense the spirit of unrest raises interesting questions about the long-debated inevitability of the revolution.[1]

The social and political breakdown that rocked Russia in 1917 had been developing for years, of course. Russia had been experiencing the growing pains of industrialization and modernization, including the growth of a working class and an industrial middle class, for decades. Its bureaucracy was simultaneously bloated and inefficient. The emancipation of the serfs in 1861 gave a boost to the country's economy, but it also struck at the heart of Russian traditional society. Meanwhile, Russia's intelligentsia—that group of educated, questioning citizens—had grown from a small cluster of privileged nobles to a much larger group that included men and women from not only the nobility but also the children of teachers, bureaucrats, priests, and lawyers. Influenced by the various strains of socialism popular in Western Europe, these intellectuals eventually began to demand the rights and freedoms of their contemporaries elsewhere. The most radical of these became

---

1 See, for example, *Was Revolution Inevitable?: Turning Points of the Russian Revolution*, Ed. Tony Brenton (New York: Oxford University Press, 2017).

revolutionaries, advocating violence to bring down the system by attacking its center, the monarchy. To that end, in 1881, a group of revolutionaries assassinated Tsar Alexander II, throwing a bomb under his carriage as it traveled through the streets of St. Petersburg. When his son Alexander III became the new tsar, he targeted the growing revolutionary movement and imposed restrictions on universities and the press. The cycle of repression and revolutionary activity continued under Alexander III's son and heir, Nicholas II.[2]

These threats to the monarchy were exacerbated by the enormous challenges on the international scene. In 1904, Russia and Japan went to war over territorial conflicts in Manchuria, ending in a humiliating defeat for Russia. It was, in part, Russia's miserable performance in the war that led to the outbreak of revolution in January 1905. After months of demonstrations and strikes, in October 1905, Nicholas realized he needed to make concessions to his angry citizens. The result was a document called the October Manifesto, which created a nationally elected consultative assembly called the Duma. Though the Duma appeared promising on paper, it actually had very limited powers and could be arbitrarily dissolved by the tsar. Consequently, though Nicholas's "compromise" may have satisfied some moderates, for others it was far too little and only intensified their revolutionary fervor.[3] Still, the monarchy continued to function, relying on the same conservative policies as always.

When war broke out in August 1914, however, the political and social strains proved too great. As Russia began to suffer defeat after defeat at the hands of the Germans, Nicholas II dismissed his commander in chief in September 1915 and took command of the troops himself. In doing so, he left his wife, Alexandra, more or less in charge, a shortsighted decision given that she was a German princess by birth and unpopular with the Russian public. By this point, there were already rumors of treason in the palace, and matters were only made worse by the royal family's attachment to the Siberian monk and self-proclaimed healer, Grigori Rasputin, who insinuated himself into the royal inner circle through his seeming ability to stop the pain and bleeding of the hemophiliac heir to the throne, Alexis. Rasputin came to serve as a spiritual advisor to the royal family and began to influence political decisions and appointments. Rasputin was murdered in December 1916, but by that

---

2 Sheila Fitzpatrick, *The Russian Revolution, 1917–1932* (Oxford: Oxford University Press, 1982), 10–26; Orlando Figes, *A People's Tragedy: The Russian Revolution, 1891–1924* (New York: Penguin Books, 1998), 3–121; See also, Philip Pomper, *The Russian Revolutionary Intelligentsia* (Arlington Heights, IL: Harlan Davidson, Inc., 1970); Richard Pipes, *The Russian Revolution* (New York: Vintage, 1991), 121–152.

3 Fitzpatrick, 26–32; Figes, 173–196; Pipes, 3–51.

time, the royal family's association with him had weakened public perception of the monarchy.[4]

Historians may argue about the primary causes of the Russian Revolution, but in the end, most would agree that it was a combination of the problems discussed above that led to the collapse of the monarchy. In late February 1917 (according to the Julian Calendar, which was still in use in Russia at the time), while Nicholas II was still at the front, demonstrations and riots broke out in Petrograd.[5] These spontaneous and unexpected demonstrations consisted of striking factory workers and housewives angry at food shortages and the continuing failures in the war. In the tsar's absence, authority crumbled, and the population of Petrograd then turned to the Duma for leadership. Recognizing the potential danger in this situation, the tsar tried to dissolve the Duma, but its members ignored his order, and on February 27, 1917, they created a Provisional Government. Nicholas attempted to return to Petrograd, but he was stranded by railroad strikes in the city of Pskov, and there, faced with the realities already described, and aware that he no longer had the support of his army commanders, Nicholas abdicated both for himself and for his son, in favor of his brother Michael. When Michael failed to accept the throne with any decisiveness, the Romanov dynasty, which had lasted over 300 years, from 1613–1917, came to an end.[6]

Over the next months, the nominal body leading Russia was the Provisional Government, but it did little to address the problems facing Russia as it planned for elections to create a true constituent assembly.[7] Meanwhile, Vladimir Lenin, the Marxist theorist and revolutionary who was eager to establish a workers' state, had already gathered a faction of followers around him under the name of the Bolsheviks. When the revolution broke out in February, Lenin was in Switzerland, but he made it clear that he opposed the Provisional Government and hoped to topple it, after which he would take Russia out of the war. Lenin soon arrived in Petrograd in early April and began to try to persuade the other Bolsheviks that it was time to stage their revolution. Lenin promised to accomplish three things once he was in

---

4 Fitzpatrick, 32–33; Figes, 246–278; Pipes, 195–232.
5 Peter the Great founded a new city, St. Petersburg, in 1703, which served as the capital for over two centuries. Then, in World War One, when Russia went to war against Germany, it decided to change the city's name, abandoning the German root for the city, "burgh," in favor of the Russian root for the city, "grad." Subsequently, after Vladimir Lenin died, the city changed its name again, to Leningrad. Finally, after the collapse of communism in 1991, the city returned to its original name of St. Petersburg.
6 Fitzpatrick, 34–60; Figes, 310–351; Pipes, 272–337.
7 Fitzpatrick, 34–60; Figes, 354–361; Pipes, 385–438.

charge: to take Russia out of the war, to distribute land to the peasantry, and to give workers control over the factories.[8] Finally, after several months, the Bolsheviks took action. On the night of October 24–25, the coup was carried out as Lenin's supporters seized the vital centers in Petrograd, such as the electricity and railroad offices. The Provisional Government held out briefly in the Winter Palace, but their defenses were inadequate and unreliable; the majority of the soldiers in Petrograd supported the Bolshevik takeover.[9]

Over the next nine months, Lenin and the Bolsheviks worked to consolidate their control and began to shape Russian life. Immediately after the coup, Lenin named himself as prime minister and Trotsky as commissar of foreign affairs and began to tackle the problems which had brought down the monarchy and the Provisional Government. The new government approved the seizing of land by peasants, placed factories in the hands of workers' committees, and issued a Decree on Peace, which called for an immediate end to the war with Germany. Shortly after, peace negotiations began in the city of Brest-Litovsk, the site of German military headquarters. Russia was not in a strong position to resist Germany's demands, and in March 1918, the two countries signed the Treaty of Brest-Litovsk. Russia lost approximately 1.3 million square miles of land, including Estonia, Latvia, Lithuania, Finland, and most of Poland; Russia also agreed to recognize Ukrainian independence.[10]

Having extracted Russia from the war, Lenin continued to consolidate his power with more and more radical measures. In March 1918, he renamed the Bolshevik Party the Communist Party, and in May, he began a program of forced grain requisitions in order to get food for the cities. In July, a new constitution placed supreme power in the All-Russian Congress of Soviets and restricted civil rights and the right to bear arms to members of the working class. By this time, however, an amalgamation of various anti-Bolshevik forces had coalesced, resulting in a civil war that would last three years. One of the most radical measures of the Bolshevik regime occurred in the first months of the Civil War, when Lenin and his new government decided to eliminate the largest remaining threat to their power, the existence of the royal family. Since April, Nicholas II and his family had been kept as prisoners, hidden away in a small house with painted-over windows in the city of Yekaterinburg, near the Ural Mountains. In July, the entire family was

---

8 Fitzpatrick, 34–60; Figes, 384–387; Pipes, 341–384.
9 Figes, 469–500; Pipes, 439–505.
10 Fitzpatrick, 34–60; Figes, 500–551; Pipes, 567–605. See also, John W. Wheeler-Bennett, *Brest-Litovsk: The Forgotten Peace, March 1918* (New York: W. W. Norton and Co.).

executed, along with their pets and several servants. The first stage of the revolution was complete.[11] None of these events seemed even remotely possible when Richard Washburn Child recorded his observations about Russia and her great potential.

Child was a man of varied talents and careers. He was born in 1881 in Massachusetts, the son of a small shop owner. He attended Harvard University as an undergraduate and published his first short story in the *Saturday Evening Post* when he was still in college. He went on to earn a law degree and opened his own law practice in 1911. His interest in writing continued throughout this period too, as he published pieces in *Ridgway's*, *McClure's*, *Collier's*, and the *Saturday Evening Post*. Shortly after, he became involved in politics, working for the Progressive Party. During the war, he worked briefly in the Treasury Department and then became the editor of *Collier's* and worked as a speechwriter for Warren G. Harding, the Republican presidential candidate. When Harding became president, he thanked Child with the ambassadorship in Rome in 1921, a position he held for three years.

Child's political leanings changed several times in his life, but he tended to be drawn to big, charismatic figures. He was especially influential in policymaking while he was ambassador to Italy, but following Harding's death, his star fell, and he struggled to find meaningful professional opportunities, despite his repeated appeals to FDR for various jobs. In 1933, he chaired the organization of the League of Republicans for Roosevelt and initially was a great supporter of FDR's spending on public works in the early days of the New Deal. But that enthusiasm quickly faded, and he soon began to criticize the cost of FDR's policies. This shift did not come as a shock to those who knew him. In the words of one historian, "His criticisms were an expression of disillusionment with the New Deal, not so much because it had failed in its promises to the country, but because it had failed in its promises to Richard Washburn Child." His initial allegiance to FDR had not led to a satisfactory appointment, and he always had a "fuzzy understanding of loyalty."[12]

His private life also floundered. Child married and divorced several times, drank too much, and worried incessantly about money. Still, in the midst of all this, he was an amazingly prolific writer, publishing over seventy articles for the *Evening Post*, as well as a number of novels and stories. He also wrote several works of nonfiction, including *Potential Russia* (1916), *Battling the Criminal* (1925), and *A Diplomat Looks at Europe* (1925). *Battling the Criminal*,

---

11 Fitzpatrick, 61–84; Figes, 556–642; Pipes, 506–565, 671–788.
12 Katy Hull, *The Machine Has a Soul: American Sympathy with Italian Fascism* (Princeton, NJ: Princeton University Press, 2021), 107–109.

in particular, is revealing of Child's view of the world. It was serialized in the *Saturday Evening Post* in 1924 and 1925 and was his attempt to explain an increase in crime in the United States. Child's position on the National Crime Commission raised his awareness of this problem, but he interpreted the issue through his own ideological lens. Child blamed juvenile delinquency on frivolous entertainment opportunities, such as bars and roadhouses; he believed that the boom in consumerism and wasteful spending, along with the transportation provided by the growing car industry, led young men astray. The result of all these shallow and meaningless pursuits was crime, amorality, and a declining work ethic.[13]

He is probably most well-known, however, for editing and publishing Benito Mussolini's autobiography. Child was a fascist sympathizer and an admirer of Mussolini, believing that the leader's actions and words revealed a certain mysticism and spiritual nature. Like many other Americans, he had a great deal of ambivalence about modernity and shared the general disillusionment after World War One that pushed so many into the arms of new, engaging ideologies like communism and fascism. He viewed "modern man" as materialistic and shallow, lacking in character, and believed that Italy was coping better with the problems of modernity than other countries. More than this, however, it may have been Child's own personality that made him attracted to fascism. One historian described him as "chauvinistic, narcissistic, and manipulative." He was xenophobic, aggressively ambitious, and "ostentatiously macho," and these personality traits predated his encounter with fascism and Mussolini.[14]

Child died of pneumonia in 1935 in Manhattan at the age of fifty-three. His papers from his time in Italy are held at the Library of Congress.[15]

Child's visit to Russia in 1916 is but one tiny piece of the much larger history of Russian-American relations. It may come as a surprise to many readers, but Russia and the United States had a good relationship for much of the nineteenth century, particularly during and after the American Civil War. Russia had refused to get involved in the Civil War, but in 1863 sent its fleet for a visit, which was interpreted by many (in the North, at least) as a sign of Russia's friendship. In 1867, Russia sold its North American territory,

---

13 Hull, 6–8, 54.
14 Hull, 3, 43, 150; Katy Hull, "Understanding Richard Washburn Child's Authoritarian Personality: From Theodor Adorno to the Histories of Gender and Emotion," *European Journal of American Studies* [Online], 18, no. 2 (Summer 2023), http://journals.openedition.org/ejas/20231.
15 "Richard Washburn Child, Onetime Lampooner, Dies," *The Harvard Crimson*, February 1, 1935.

soon to be known as Alaska, to the United States. Four years later, the tsar's son, Grand Duke Alexis, toured the United States for three months, meeting many of the top political, cultural, and scientific figures of the day and touring America's cities and national wonders. During this period, consequently, there was a general perception that America and Russia were friends, and there was an effort to highlight their similarities, such as their respective abolitions of serfdom and slavery in the 1860s. At the end of the nineteenth and beginning of the twentieth century, however, as the Russian monarchy became more oppressive in the wake of the assassination of Alexander II at the hands of terrorists, this rosy view of Russian-American relations faltered. In this new climate, American activists embarked upon a crusade to free Russia from the religious persecution and political tyranny of the tsarist empire. Russia's famine of 1891–1892 had already caused many Americans to assess the Russian government, if not the Russian people, more harshly. Another issue that dampened the ardor of the United States for Russia was the latter nation's treatment of its Jewish population. In 1903, after the violent pogrom at Kishinev, Ukraine, the U.S. government under Theodore Roosevelt even agreed to send a petition signed by prominent citizens from around the country to Nicholas II, inquiring about the condition of Jews in that region. Ultimately, the Russian government would not receive it.[16]

Child was far from the first American to be fascinated by the enormous nation straddling Europe and Asia. Some of these admirers were interested in Russian literature or art; others were curious about the emerging socialist movement in Russia. Child's intended purpose was to go beyond the news articles that kept the American people informed about the progress of the great war. Child declared that he went to Europe, and particularly Russia, "to see what war is doing to the hearts of men and the spirit of nations." He believed that Russia was a country that would be greatly transformed by the war and that it would be remade. In writing this book, he wished to convey that Russia possessed a wealth of yet-to-be-realized possibilities. In Russia, Child saw "the awakening of a nation; the promise of a new social era; the beginning of a development of vast human, material, and spiritual resource [...] the like of which does not exist" (Chapter 1). As an introduction to the Russian people and their nature, Child paints a romantic portrait

---

16 Lee A. Farrow, *Seward's Folly: A New Look at the Alaska Purchase* (Fairbanks, AK: University of Alaska Press, 2017) and *Alexis in America: A Grand Duke's Tour, 1871–1872* (Baton Rouge, LA: LSU Press, 2014). Regarding American attitudes toward Russia later, see, for example, David Foglesong, *The American Mission and the "Evil Empire"* (Cambridge: Cambridge University Press, 2007), and David Engerman, *Modernization from the Other Shore* (Cambridge: Harvard University Press, 2003).

of Russian life and sacrifice through a fictional peasant named Maxim. Blond and sturdy, Maxim displays the traits of piety, simplicity, and resilience. Eventually, Maxim is called upon to fight for his country and, like so many other young men, dies in anonymity. Though modern readers may find Child's story of Maxim to be a bit clichéd, one contemporary review praised the book for its vividness and emotion in "its presentation of the more hopeful and human side of the Russian people."[17]

Child also sought to address misconceptions about Russia, explaining that Russia was a country of "contradictions and rumors." Though the government was a strict autocracy, the people had a strong sense of individualism: "nowhere, certainly not in the United States, is there such a democracy of human feeling." Child admired the Russian people: "the real Russian—the Russian of the millions—is a person of wonderful sweetness of soul and knows how to live skillfully, even under difficulties, a simple, pure, and gentle life." He believed that Russia and its people had been misrepresented and misunderstood as a consequence of a paucity of information.

Child arrived after Tsar Nicholas II had decided to take charge of the troops. Child admired the Tsar and hoped that a clearer picture of him would facilitate friendly relations between America and Russia. He describes the royal family in favorable tones but also addresses the problematic rumors about Rasputin and his power at court. Though claiming not to be an advocate of prohibition, Child praises Nicholas's abolition of the State Vodka Monopoly at the outbreak of the war, calling it the "miracle measure." There had already been a temperance movement in Russia prior to the war, but the mobilization of forces in 1914 pushed Nicholas into action, leading him to ban all vodka sales. In doing so, he eliminated a third of the state's revenue at a critical moment. Child calls prohibition "so beneficent, so extraordinary in effect, from which the results in a short space of time have been so marked and so cumulative," and credits it with a list of improvements, ranging from a more efficient army to "better babies." In fact, the ban on vodka did not stop alcohol consumption entirely, as the desperate and creative resorted to moonshine, smuggling, or drinking inferior and dangerous substitutes, such as shoe polish, cologne, and varnish.[18]

---

17 Review of *Potential Russia* in *The North American Review*, 204, no. 730 (September 1916), 464–466.
18 Patricia Herlihy, "The Russian Vodka Prohibition of 1914 and Its Consequences," in *Dual Markets: Comparative Approaches to Regulation*, edited by Ernesto U. Savona, Mark A. R. Kleiman, and Francesco Calderoni (Cham: Springer, 2017).

Child admits that all is not perfect in Russia. The country suffered from a lack of industrial development, incompetence, and a shortage of accessible ports. But Child was dismayed by the exaggerated reports of bribes and corruption and blamed the rumors on foreign commercial representatives looking to pad their own pockets with inflated expense reports.

Child also discusses the horrors of the war in Russia—the hordes of refugees fleeing their destroyed villages in the hope of finding food and shelter and the cities, overwhelmed by this influx of the needy. But even in these descriptions, Child often turns suffering into material for his charming and romantic portrayal of the peasants. With their pink cheeks, wrinkled faces, and colorful makeshift winter clothing, the peasant refugees were "picturesque [...] a band, not only of tragedy, but also of romance, because it was more itinerant than the gypsies and its end was more unreal and mythical and mysterious than the pot of gold behind the rainbow." Moreover, rather than focusing on the death and destruction, Child highlights the "reawakened spirit of the brotherhood of man" and the "communal spirit of the refugees" that appeared despite the necessity of self-preservation. His insistence on the silver lining in war may strike modern readers as naïve and offensive; for example, Child's summary of the state of the Russian common people:

> The refugees suffer. But the refugees learn to know the spirit which lies deep down within them. And the refugees are only a fraction of the people of Russia. The rest of the Russian people because of the refugees are learning to know themselves. They are sensing the revival of social consciousness, they are acting the prologue before a new era of recognition of a spiritual life.

Child's observations often lack nuance. He dedicates a chapter to Russian women, which, interestingly enough, was true of several other chroniclers of the period. The role of women was, at the time, being discussed internationally, as the question of giving women suffrage was a source of debate and conflict.[19] In many countries involved in the war, women had stepped up to take the jobs left behind by men. Russia's women, Child argues, are extraordinarily important, and "her progress and her potentiality are so interwoven with the progress and potentiality of her country that the story of the woman

---

19 For example, Princess Julia Cantacuzène, *Russian People: Revolutionary Recollections* (Americans in Revolutionary Russia), with an introduction and annotations by Norman Saul (Bloomington, IN: Slavica, 2017); Louise Bryant, *Six Red Months in Russia*, with an introduction and annotations by Lee A. Farrow (Bloomington, IN: Slavica, 2017).

parallels the story of the war-awakened Russian people." At the same time, he also judges women on their appearance: "Russian women are not pretty; many are ugly, but they have that beauty of active minds and excellent hearts which shines forth. The modern Russian woman has not much art in dress." He does, however, praise them for their eagerness to obtain education and recognize Russia's superiority in this area.

His characterization of the Russians as "Oriental" may be similarly troubling for modern readers, though he is not alone in using this term. Many others who chronicled visits to Russia before him referred to the "Orientalism" or "Oriental fatalism" of the Russians, in most cases without really explaining what these traits might be. Child echoes these stereotypes and describes what he observes as "primitive" and "Oriental" behavior in trading: using an abacus, bartering at length, and delaying—"They say, "Tomorrow, tomorrow," as if they were above being hurried by vulgar business."

Child's overall assessment of Russia, however, is overwhelmingly positive and optimistic. He finds great promise in Russia's abundant natural resources—a large population of potential laborers, timber, farmland, and mineral deposits. He believes that Russia will emerge from the war better and stronger, ready to be developed and engaged in international trade. He observes that Britain is already recognizing Russia's potential, noting the establishment of a Russian Section in the British Chamber of Commerce in London. His call to action expresses both urgency and incredulity, pleading with the United States to recognize the possibilities that would emerge through a better understanding of Russia before those opportunities are exploited by other nations. Child stresses the importance of effective diplomacy and the appointment of a capable and forward-thinking ambassador, one who can speak Russian and understands the Russian way of doing business. Child credits the Germans for recognizing these key elements long before other countries did: "Germany did not only invade the Russian market with the patience and efficiency of its individual manufacturers and sell agencies but she did more—she *organized*, for the Russian business."

Child concludes his book about Russia with a hopeful prediction of what Americans will gain from their interactions with and explorations of the Russians and their culture—an opportunity for self-examination through the eyes of another people. Specifically, Americans might discover that their "complicated material civilization is not only a failure, but perhaps an instrument of blight. [...] Knowing Russia will not only be good for the tired business man's profit; it will also be good for his soul." His message about Russia seems to anticipate Child's own awakening and his philosophical shift away from American capitalism and toward Italian fascism, which would occur just a few years later.

Chapter 1

BETWEEN YESTERDAY AND TOMORROW

The things which one can see and hear in the din and chaos of the world's greatest war are many, lurid, picturesque, quaint, humorous, heroic, and horrible but by themselves and without inquiry as to where they came from or to what they are leading, they are not of first consequence.

From the fighting front much detail of modern war is seen as through a microscope, and from the capitals of the nations the broad canvas of international struggle is seen as through a telescope. But having gone to scenes of this conflict and having been among its terrible mysteries, I know that from afar - in America - may be collected the most detail, because of the flood of written description, photographs and moving pictures from all sources, and that as from a mountaintop, without the prejudices of the arena itself, America may see with clearer perspective the great and changing picture.

I have seen men who had been shot to pieces in barbed wire entanglements, and I was with Lord Robert Cecil[1] in the British Foreign Office when the news of the execution in Belgium of Miss Cavell[2] came in, and later I discussed with prominent Englishmen the effect which the execution would have upon the sympathies and opinions of the world. I cannot see that I gained

---

1 Lord Robert Cecil (1864-1958) was a British lawyer and diplomat who was one of the architects of the League of Nations after World War One, advocating for the use of the recently-created universal language called Esperanto in the League. He earned a Nobel Peace Prize in 1937 for his service to that organization. He was also a critic of German appeasement in the interwar years.
2 Edith Cavill (1865-1915) was a British nurse who had been serving as the matron of a school for nurses in Brussels, Belgium, for several years when World War One broke out. She stayed and continued to work even after Germany had occupied Belgium, caring for both Belgian and German soldiers, but in 1915, she was accused of assisting Allied soldiers in leaving the country to rejoin the fight. The Germans arrested her and executed her by firing squad on October 12, 1915. Her execution intensified anti-German sentiment in both Britain and the United States. She is remembered with a statue near Trafalgar Square in London.

anything by being present at either occasion. The spinster on a New England farm can imagine perfectly how dead men look when piled up in a gully; the New York elevator boy could estimate more correctly than Berlin or London the effect upon the opinions of the world of the execution of Miss Cavell.

Well it is that these things are chronicled and pictured; but I did not go to Europe, and especially to Russia, without a wish to do more than to chronicle and picture. Primarily I went to see what war is doing to the hearts of men and the spirit of nations. Russia, I believed, was the place where the war would work the greatest changes.

I went to Russia not to look back too much upon old Russia, but forward a little at Russia as a great potentiality. I wished that I might stand without wobbling between yesterday and tomorrow, and if my book has any reason for being, it lies in this attempt.

The war has mystified us and stupefied us. So now more than ever there seems to me to be a need for eyes that can look both forward and back, and a discretion that can choose the significant facts from those of less consequence no matter how startling these latter may be, and a carefulness not to let our desires for the future distort the truth about the present and the past, or the real nature of man.

When I was in Russia I had a definite desire to see the war and its effect as my acquaintance with two men - Theodore Roosevelt and Edward Mandell House[3] - had led me to believe they would see the war and its effect upon Russia. I believe these men, different as they are, to be the two greatest living Americans; I think they stand apart from most men because they see yesterdays widely and tomorrows forward. The contrast of these two men with other Americans serves to emphasize the rarity of this combined backward and forward vision, so important to us now when we can no longer maintain a seclusion from world politics. Elihu Root, for example, is often said to be the "ablest man in America."[4] Few will deny that he sees the yesterdays of the world with extraordinary vision, but William Jennings Bryan[5] might say that

---

3 Edward Mandell House (1858-1938) was an American diplomat who served as an advisor to Woodrow Wilson and one of the five American commissioners at the Paris Peace Conference.
4 Elihu Root (1845–1937) was the former US secretary of war and state who led a special commission, often referred to as the Root Commission, that was charged with investigating the economic and political situation in Russia in order to make recommendations to President Woodrow Wilson on ways that the United States could assist Russia. The United States sup- ported the priority of the Allies on the Western Front.
5 William Jennings Bryan (1860-1925) was an American lawyer, orator, and politician who ran for President three times on the Democratic ticket. He served in Congress

Root's sincere and almost ardent attempts to see and feel tomorrow, as for instance, Louis D. Brandeis[6] sees and feels tomorrow, are pathetic.

Bryan, on the other hand, sees a vision of tomorrow. But Elihu Root might say that Bryan fails to see and know yesterday and today. He might point out as William Hard,[7] one of the competent contributors to periodicals, has said, that Bryan only knows a world as he prefers to have it, and that the past and present of Bryan's world is one which exists only in the preference of Bryan.

Because men like House and Roosevelt are wise enough to look backward and see a world as it is, and not a world as they would prefer to have it, and at the same hour can look forward toward tomorrow, it was of them and their viewpoint I thought when I was in Russia, and when I was preparing this book.

And I thought of them again when I talked with Henry Ford in Europe, because whatever may be the difference between Roosevelt and House, the difference between them and Ford is somewhat greater. It was Henry Ford's belief, just as it was Miss Jane Addams'[8] belief, that the "boys in the trenches" were there against their wills, or because of hate. Ford and Miss Addams preferred to believe this, and preferring to believe this, they believed it by preference. They are lovable in their wish for a better, sweeter, and less savage world. The difficulty is that they base conclusions upon the hypotheses directly contrary to the fact that the "boys in the trenches" are not there against their wills or because of hate, but are there because of their cooperative and combined wills and because of their love for something not themselves - a love so great that they will give their lives for it.

This fact I believe is true - even in Russia. Russia has a past, and it will fill many hundreds of books of this size. Russia has a present, and it is horrible

---

and as Secretary of State under Woodrow Wilson, but is probably best known for his famous "Cross of Gold" speech in 1896 during the debates over the American monetary standard and for his role in the Scopes Trial as an opponent of the teaching of evolution in schools.

6 Louis D. Brandeis (1856-1941) was an enormously important figure in American jurisprudence, the first Jewish attorney on the Supreme Court, and a strong advocate for freedom of speech.
7 William Hard (1878-1962) was a journalist and social reformer who was a resident of Jane Addams' Hull House.
8 Jane Addams (1860-1935) was an activist and social reformer best known for her leadership in the settlement house movement of the late nineteenth and early twentieth century, founding Hull House in Chicago in 1889. The goal of these settlements was to provide education and aid to immigrants and industrial workers. During World War One, she also became vocal in the international peace movement. In 1931, she won the Nobel Peace Prize.

with war, as I have tried to show. But Russia has a future and it is great, and it is most important of all. Russia is changing. Bad as war may be, it does much for man. War takes lives in vast numbers and with comic ghastliness; war scorches the surface of a land like Poland, and all is black, charred and horrible; war leaves the survivors torn in heart, and, I am told, future generations weak in body. War makes men frightful. But it also makes them saints.

When all is said against war there still remains the fact that men and women often enter war for the good of their souls and the souls of their kind, and this good they gain. From this point of view it means nothing to me that they have or have not been deceived as to the cause of war by their rulers; it means nothing to me whether the cause in my opinion, differing from theirs perhaps, is good or bad. War, as I have seen war, and especially war in Russia, transfigures mankind. When nothing else has come to teach men and women that property or life itself is not their most dear possession, war may come to snatch the cover from the souls of men. And whether we would prefer to believe it or not, war teaches man that he is willing to die for a bit of colored ribbon, if he believes, rightly or wrongly, that that bit of ribbon represents the good of his kind. If he did not believe that there was something more dear than life, he would not believe in God.

I for one, coming back from Russia, more than ever wish to cast my lot with those who have faith that a nation of survivors of an ideal, is better than a world full of personal property and personal preservations. Peace is sweet if it costs the spirit nothing, but if peace exacts a tribute from the spirit, then war, and not peace, is glorious and kind.

"It is not a ruble in the hand nor the heart in a breast which counts," said a Russian soldier to me; "only Russia - Russia of our Creator." This is the spirit from which nations are made; this is the spirit upon which the future of man depends, not only for the flicker light of a life, but for eternity.

This is the spirit which is rising from war; it is remaking Russia.

There were horrible things to be seen in Russia. Of these I thought the tragedy of the refugees, and the terrible slaughter of soldiers which cannot be paralleled elsewhere, were the two things which best showed how fearful modern war may become.

But in Russia today there is also the awakening of a nation; the promise of a new social era; the beginning of a development of a vast human, material, and spiritual resource. This undeveloped resource, the like of which does not exist, belongs not only to Russia, but to the world.

These are the things I desire that this book shall show.

Chapter 2

CANNON MEAT

One instance is the case of Maxim. The story of Maxim will tell much of Russia at war. With its movement, its color, and its pictures it will contain much of the sum total that one can see or feel in the empire of the Czar today. In it there is the theme of the fourth of the four great dramatic facts of this conflict.

The first of these great dramatic facts, I think, is the spirit of Great Britain. No empire has ever been given the free-will service of so many men willing, if need be, to die. I spoke to a Scotland Yard secret-service man in Norway of the millions of British volunteers. "You were in England!" said he. "You saw it." He spoke as if it were a vision.

And the second is the efficiency of Germany. I have been in five countries, and two of them are Germany's bitterest enemies. But even where anti-Prussianism is almost madness, whether among statesmen and officials, those who fight and those who wait, or those who fear and those who have suffered, there is mingled in one breath hatred and admiration.

And the third is the dignity of France. This, too, is felt everywhere. At the cold, narrow gate of Russia, on the frontier between Finland and Sweden, I met General Pau[1] on his way to visit the Czar's army. This distinguished veteran officer of France, one-armed and not tall of stature, behind his heavy gray brows and white mustache has a countenance filled with a strange combination of power and sadness. That which is firm and resolute and that which is reflective and tender mingle in the expression of his features. I spoke of the dignity of France, and then feared I had taken too great a liberty and had changed too abruptly from some hurried words about the Russian army, whose General Staff headquarters I had just left. He smiled, however, quietly and with pleasure. "France is patient and strong," he said. "If necessary, she

---

[1] General Paul Pau (1848-1932) had served in the Franco-Prussian War, where he lost part of his arm. At the start of World War One, he came out of retirement to serve again, first as commander of an army and then as the French representative to the Russian high command.

will suffer without complaint, but also she will remain calm after her victories." The Russian commandant of the frontier station looked at Pau with blinking eyes and wet his own lips with the tip of his tongue. But he said nothing.

And the fourth drama of the conflict concerns a terrible thing. It is the human flesh of the endless hordes of men. It is the stockyard hordes of armies like the Russian army. It is the story of the millions. But, individually, it is the story of Maxim.

Russia is a country of peasants; if Maxim were destined to be born in Russia the chances were three to one that he would be a peasant, and that Maxim should be a peasant fate decreed. Fate dropped him, a pink and squirming thing, in a little Russian village a day's journey from Petrograd, and almost that distance from Moscow.

Maxim represented Russia as much as any soul could represent Russia. He was more Russian than the Czar, more Russian than any bureaucrat. He was a Slav, a peasant; he was one of the 120,000,000 cast in the image of God and tilling the soil. More than this, his infancy represented Russia because the lusty health of his young flesh combined with the stare of his blue eyes, in which no one could quite tell whether there were simplicity or guile, dense ignorance or the ancient meditations of old Oriental mysteries.[2] Above all, Maxim had the quality which is the essence of the charm of Russia and Russia's peasantry. It was not picturesqueness; it was not simplicity or elusiveness: it was potentiality, it was possibility. Like Russia, Maxim was a humanized question mark; he was a slate upon which nothing had been written. No one could tell whether he was the world's yesterday or the world's tomorrow.

He was born into a world of earth and wood. And in this, too, he represented Russia, for Russia is a civilization of earth and wood. That which satisfies the hunger of the Russian mind is ownership of soil; it is the passion of the empire. That which satisfies the hunger of his body is eaten with a wooden spoon from a wooden bowl.

The home of Maxim, for whom destiny has marked out a part - a little but significant part - in the great world war, was of wood. Snow and wind from the lowering skies of Russian winters had turned to weathered gray the unpainted exterior of the half-thatched peasant home, the roof of which extended to cover the shed in which the horse, the two cows, and a pig were kept. Inside, in the room where Maxim, his sister, and his father and mother spent all of their indoor hours, the reverse side of the lumber was yellow-brown, unplastered, and undecorated, except by clothes that hung on the

---

2 Many visitors to Russia have commented on the "Orientalism" of Russians.

wall, by four covers of a magazine published in Moscow, wooden utensils on a shelf, and a painted wooden icon hung in the corner so that a saint of the Russian orthodox church might ever cast upon the room a benevolent stare from brown, doe-like eyes. There was a large wooden table and a stove of tiles with a mouth always hungry for wood.

The outdoor world across which the young legs of Maxim first began to walk was a part of the great Russian plain, but the village of fourteen or fifteen houses was built under the shadows of four lines of birch trees, whose leafy tops waved the summer, so that the birches writhed as gracefully as dancing dryads - as the birches wave in a landscape by Corot. Maxim's world extended as time went on and as his hair grew more and more like flax through the bleaching of hatless summers, and then, as his body was made to have magnificent form and strength, retaining its unbent, untwisted youth through its labor in the communal fields, extended until this world of his could be said to include nearly thirty square miles. It included at least one town on the railroad from which the produce of the countryside was shipped away and in which there were such things as newspapers from Petrograd and Moscow, and a local government in the control of landed proprietors which was a cross between a paternal village-improvement association and a board of aldermen, was called a zemstvo council, and maintained schools, doctors, and hospitals. Maxim did not know that a few years ago only one person in four in Russia could read or write; it was quite a normal thing not to read or write, but Maxim learned from a traveling teacher because a plump, young thing named Vera, who looked most pretty in the old peasant heirloom dress, had learned and teased Maxim unmercifully for his backwardness. If he could have foreseen the Great War, no doubt he would not have bothered his head; for, like the millions of him, Maxim was something of, a simple philosopher.

He was something of a simple philosopher, but his religion had a large part in the sweetness of his life. In Maxim there was a capacity for religious feeling of which even Father Sergius, the village priest, a rather stupid man, did not dream. Maxim's world was small, therefore the unknown world of superstition and of religious hope appeared all the larger. The young man saw that men of his own age in the town celebrated holidays by their vodka drinking and congregated in tough gangs - a new thing in Russia - but it was Maxim and not these tough young men of the town who could represent the spirit of the Russian peasantry. Maxim simply prayed for help and purity and for the pity of a stern God; his eyes remained clear as crystals from the Urals, and there was a spring in his step as he walked over the creaking snow in his rope and basket shoes, his padded leg swathings, and his calf-skin cap, and he had deep-breathing lungs and coursing blood under his skin.

In this respect, too, he represented the real, human Russia. An American doctor in charge of one of the largest of the hospitals, receiving soldiers from the front, told me that among the six thousand muzhiks[3] he had treated only eleven men had the diseases of immorality. "Why?" said I. "Russian peasant: religion, clean living," said he. "I never believed an army could be so free from these diseases."

In the winter the young man's father went to the city where, as an izvoshchik, or single-horse public vehicle driver, in a padded coat, he earned money, not to spend upon luxuries, but with the eternal Russian muzhik's ambition, his land madness: the same land madness which forced the abolition of serfdom in Russia and which, way down deep, consuming the Russian heart, was the real strength behind the agitation of the so-called intelligent class in cities and towns and the urban revolutionary elements that in 1905 resulted in Russia's first Duma or national assembly: a form, if not a fact, of constitutional government. The theory of constitutional government Maxim did not understand at all, and in this respect he represented the real Russia much better than the universities and the widely diverse reform theories and the politicians of the cities. But he understood the land madness of the muzhiks, for he had it.

Maxim had also a Slav sense of a mild sort. Between himself and his own customs and the peasants and the customs of villages not far away there were vast differences. In common, however, there were Slav instincts, the orthodox religion, the vague, mysterious recognition of a vague, mysterious government, and at bottom a childlike attitude toward the Czar which has given rise to the term Little Father. All these combined bound Maxim to other Russians, to the infinite world of Russia beyond the horizon of his own little world.

Happy enough, dreaming much, worshiping blindly, in ignorance of the modern western world, but feeling a hunger for it; not influenced much by the Orient, but feeling its ancient breath, Maxim, the human animal whose body was beautiful, whose hair was light, and whose mind was dark, still represented Russia, for he was young, strong, rather inscrutable, untested, undeveloped - a Potentiality.

Then the war came. The news of the war reached the village, but in the length and breadth of that little hamlet no one could be found who knew why the war had come. War was something which came like a tempest of unknown forces. Not even the zemstvo doctor who came into the canton could explain. A war was in progress, and that was a fact to be accepted, for

---

3 The Russian word for peasant.

the mind of the muzhik likes to say to itself: "Life is life; a fact is a fact, and if nothing can be done about it, it is something to be taken down in one gulp." Old Vladimir, who heard that the Czar was fighting the Austrians, recalled the days he had spent in Petrograd and said: "Well, the Germans are a great business people, and it is lucky they are on our side." It took several days to correct the impression which the remark had made. Indeed, it was not until Vera had received a note sent by a messenger from her brother, who was serving his term in the army, that it was known that the Russian forces had been mobilized and that the western frontier already was in the tumult of masses of men and metal hurled against other masses of men and metal in a fury of hate which no one understood.

One evening Maxim came back from a journey to the town on the railroad. Summer had gone, and the skies, with their flat, gray blanket threatening a winter covering for the flat Russian plains, were lit for a moment in the west with a flare of red as if the war had thrown up the spray of its blood and fire. Maxim plodded along beside the undersized chestnut horse with the flax-colored mane and tail, but the head of the young man was bowed and his mind was full of the pictures he had seen.

At the railroad station of the town a troop train had stopped and out of it there had poured in liquid streams endless soldiers, unshaven, unbathed, red-eyed. It was a Siberian regiment which had marched and ridden and starved and thirsted across the empire. The men were strange types, and in the last cars of the train were half a hundred tribesmen from the far eastern borders of Mongolia who wore jackets of sheepskin with the wool side exposed and fierce, curved knives carried in broad metal-studded belts. Maxim had thought that the enemies of Russia had arrived, for he did not know that beside the body of the army, made up of muzhiks, the fighting strength of Russia contains much wilder and more curious elements than the Cossacks. He did not know that some of these strange tribesmen ask after a few hours of their journey from their homes when the fighting will begin, and that in one case, over a hundred miles from the Austro-German trenches, some of these tribesmen roamed abroad by night and, returning, reported to the Russian officers that they had killed seven Japanese, but that four had escaped.

Maxim had seen the flat cars carrying the field pieces; and he wondered if these had been cast from the metal which once had been the chimes in the church of the town and which the authorities had taken away. He knew nothing about the great Russian standing army which the Government was to throw headlong without sufficient munitions into the hungry mouth of the slaughter, day after day, until that active army of more than two millions would be wiped out and it would be the turn of the reserves.

When the troop train of the Siberians had gone Maxim could see the second train standing on the other track. A great crowd was around it, and yet he could see that a truck was being moved from car to car and that limp men were being taken out of the doors and placed in double rows. "They are hurt!" gasped Maxim, standing on tiptoe. "They are dead," answered the crowd, it seemed almost joyfully, and a cloud of its breath showed on the frosty air. "I am so glad I am not twenty-one, the army age," said Maxim. "I would have to be killed."

But that night, when he had entered the living room of his father's cottage, he hung upon the wall a picture which he had bought. It was the colored lithograph of a man unbelievably handsome and perfect, the portrait of a demigod. It was a picture familiar all over Russia. It is supposed to be the likeness of the Czar.

Maxim during the ten months that followed often came in from work in the fields and looked at the icon in the corner, crossing himself, and at the picture of the Czar. The icon meant God, and the Czar meant Russia, and he knew in a general way that Russia was threatened; that his own kind was threatened. He knew no more of why there was a war than he knew in the beginning. Austrian prisoners had gone by in open freight cars with the cold rain beating down upon their bedraggled, muddy uniforms, and their heads, often hatless and matted, bowed down in hopeless misery. One of them had looked at Maxim, and Maxim had waved his hand because he felt the sense of being a human creature and that the other was a human creature too. But the prisoner from a long distance spat at Maxim.

"God will take care of Russia," said Maxim. "I hope I will not have to fight." In these words he spoke something of the presence of fanaticism and the lack of an intelligent patriotism in Russia: Maxim was still being representative of human Russia, the overwhelming peasant Russia. But Maxim had to fight. After the notice a soldier came. "Do you know what you are now?" said the soldier, and a scar on his cheek grew red as he said it. "You are what we call cannon meat."

Chapter 3
ALL FOR RUSSIA

From childhood Maxim had felt the presence of some mysterious authority over his destiny. Somewhere there was a government. Its arm was long; its grasp was strong; its power was great. If it now reached out for Maxim at a time when the harvest was just beginning, and, indeed, at the time when he was making plans to marry Vera, the niece of old Vladimir, there was nothing to be done about it. So it is in Russia. But also there is an astonishing self-respect for the individual in Russia; so strong is it that in many quarters parents and school-teachers would not think of corporal punishment. Therefore Maxim looked at the recruiter, who was old enough to be his father, and said insolently: "You make a good soldier." The other looked at Maxim's clear skin and eyes, at his flaxen hair, and at the straight, powerful body of the young giant. "So do you," he said indulgently. "And when you are a soldier you will learn something about your country. When soldiers come back from wars they are the wisest men in their villages. And they can talk of things that no one can print in newspapers."

Maxim was glad to hear it. He put a map of Russia on the wall and made the soldier draw a line upon it to show his old father, bent by husbandry, and his old mother, withered by housewifery and hoeing cabbages, where the fighting was going on. "Warsaw has fallen," said the soldier. "I know. I can read," replied Maxim. "If the people would pray more, we would get it back again."

His mother's knotted fingers clung to his sleeve, and her thin, dry lips were shut tight. Vera cried a little and allowed herself the torture of memories of spring days when they had danced together outdoors on the green behind the communal steam bathhouse. So Maxim left his village with his young, strong body and his good, untrained mind and a woolen blouse, a woolen suit, and a pair of greased boots; with him he took all that he had.

The eggshell of his narrow world had burst. In a daze and a dream the dirty old passenger car whisked him through the sleepless night, crowded among other young men whose lips had just begun to show a growth of hair and who chattered ceaselessly about the war and their own villages and new rumors until drowsiness and stupor overcame them. They were all muzhiks gathered up for the service of the Czar. Maxim stared at their shadowy outlines in the dim light of the one candle at the end of the car, the rays of which were reflected on the gilt of an icon at the other end. But for the most part he pressed the end of his straight nose against the windowpane, watching the showering sparks from the wood-burning locomotive and the villages which flashed by, lying dark against the white film of moonlight on the fields.

The next day was the most noteworthy of all his life, thought Maxim, for the train had taken him to Petrograd, the capital of his country! This was a place of dreams indeed! Out of the train tumbled all the new recruits, and they were marched down the Nevsky Prospect[1] as far as the Liteyny Prospect,[2] grinning at the wonderful life on the great capital thoroughfare, at the unbelievable buildings, monuments, and shops; gayly uniformed coachmen, beautiful ladies, and soldiers in many uniforms; Cossacks in gay cloaks and dashing, prancing horses; officers with tinkling medals and clanking swords; the Cathedral of Our Lady of Kazan,[3] and gilded domes and spires.

Only once did Maxim, breathless with wonder and fear, laugh. This was when he saw himself and the others turn the street corner into the gloomier avenue. The petty officer in uniform ran forward and turned the leaders as a shepherd turns the course of animals; it was exactly as if the men had been a flock of sheep or a herd of cattle. There all went past numerous Red Cross signs, denoting hospitals or the wounded from the front, on to the military barracks. And there Maxim was given a uniform, shoes, and belt. They were the best clothes he had ever had; to him they seemed to be a gift from the Czar, a personal gift, and when he had an opportunity to observe himself in a mirror he was filled with vain thoughts which may have been forgiven because, like the millions, Maxim, in his visored cap and his long frieze coat, with his broad shoulders, ample chest, hard, clean cheeks, and well-shaven chin was a magnificent picture of a soldier. And he, the humble muzhik Maxim, had gazed upon the great red buildings of government around the open space where stands the towering column of Alexander the First, and had seen the palace of the Czar, and canal boats passing under the Nikolai Bridge when the sunset was reflected on the River Neva!

---

1 Nevsky Prospect runs through the center of St. Petersburg.
2 Liteyny Prospect is another major street in the center of St. Petersburg; it runs perpendicular to Nevsky Prospect.
3 Built between 1801 and 1811, Kazan Cathedral is a spectacular cathedral on Nevsky Prospect, the main street that runs through the heart of St. Petersburg.

They taught Maxim to be a soldier. Who were They! They were the Government. They were the man above the man above the man above. They were Authority. That is who They were. Maxim did not understand it very well. He was told that They were the bureaucracy under the Czar. There were ministers and ranks or grades or *chins*, as they are called, and some were dishonest and some were incompetent, so that, at any rate, it made a very stupid, clumsy machine which did little rather badly and did that little with slowness. But, in any case, there was nothing to be done about it. The peasants were making Russia, and those who were ruling Russia were much more intelligent than the peasants, and besides They were They, and Maxim was only Maxim.

So, under the Ministry of War, there were ranks in the army too, descending to the man who drilled the squad in which Maxim learned to be a soldier and fight with a "3-line" rifle to which a bayonet is fixed permanently. Maxim took the drilling seriously except on rare occasions when he felt a temptation to laugh. On these occasions, when the company to which he belonged and other companies were engaged in marching and practicing the manual of arms in the square before the Cathedral of St. Isaac,[4] where the grim, sullen, and vandalized German Embassy stands stripped of its decorations by a mob, or in Dvortsovy Square,[5] or on the great Field of Mars, upon which the slanting sun sometimes tries to throw the shadows of the cupolas of the Church of the Resurrection,[6] the men cast in the image of God suddenly seemed to be cattle or sheep, herded and driven. And Maxim would laugh to himself at the idea.

To him, a peasant, the new world of Petrograd and eternal drill, drill, drill was a dream world. Everything in it was confusingly wonderful, and nothing in it was real. He never knew there were so many men in the world as he saw being made into soldiers. Companies and regiments which had been in training for weeks and weeks disappeared every few days and new squads appeared. The new squads came in by day, and the old disappeared during the night, marching silently through side streets toward the railroads with their guns and their equipment. Word was passed around that Russia would swamp her enemies by the number and the courage of her men, and

---

4 Built in the mid-nineteenth century, St. Isaac's Cathedral is a large Orthodox church in St. Petersburg. Its notable features include enormous malachite columns in its interior.
5 Palace Square, at the end of Nevsky Prospect in St. Petersburg, is the location of the Winter Palace, the former residence of the royal family (currently, the Hermitage art museum).
6 This church, which stylistically resembles the more famous St. Basil's Cathedral in Moscow, is located on the site of the assassination of Alexander II by terrorists in 1881.

confidence was manufactured by a government which had failed to manufacture shrapnel. If Americans and other foreigners could be taken down to the Russian winter front and cajoled into believing that the Russian army was in shape to sweep over into Austria, regaining all her lost territory, it is no wonder that Maxim, with his blind faith in a Russia loving God and the Slav power, believed that he was an infinitesimal unit in the millions who would know great victories.

The swing of the Russian marching step began to rise from his feet to enter his brain. The sound of the band stirred his blood. He saw the Imperial Cossack Guard practicing cavalry charges on the Field of Mars, and he believed that nothing could withstand such sword-drawn onslaughts. Winter had come, and the Summer Garden, with its granite urns and its strange, deserted acres, was covered with the same snow that creaked beneath his feet; but now drilling, bayonet practice in which lunges were made at bundles of straw, called by some of the soldiers "Kaiser Wilhelms," and singing songs in the barracks were all parts of a new life, a dream life, an intoxicated life, a life of the drunken emotions.

And then, suddenly one night, there were secret orders. The company of peasant soldiers of which Maxim was one were moved hurriedly from their barracks. No one knew why. Maxim, at the station, watched the men being divided into squads and put into box cars. He laughed because in the railroad town near his village he had seen stock animals driven up inclined runways into freight cars in the same way.

He remembered in the night that during the mobilization period of the Russo-Japanese War, he, as a boy, had seen soldiers in a train of box cars, and in his young way he had realized then that the stalled train, with its drunken soldiers falling out of the doors and lying helpless in the ditches, meant that vodka had rendered helpless soldiers, railroad men, locomotive engineers, and all. He was glad that the Little Father had put an end to this. Now vodka seldom appeared among the soldiers: only when some doctor had sold a pint for many rubles.

In the afternoon the train had reached Mogilev, and somebody told Maxim that Mogilev was the place where the Russian General Staff, the Czar's staff, had its headquarters. The new regiment was to take the place of an older regiment gone to the front. In Mogilev one could smell war: there was the faint odor of blood and smokeless powder. White-capped nurses of the Red Cross came and went, and doctors and squads of prisoners. A watchman on the high white tower balcony surveyed the picturesque central Russian town and could look down on companies of soldiers who went through narrow streets singing stirring songs on their way to their bath; he could see the

Czar's residence surrounded by sentry boxes and the guards, all in white fur, hugging their guns in the cold.

The Czar came and went in secrecy to and from Mogilev and Petrograd, and Maxim never caught a single glance at him, but once he saw General Alexiev,[7] the Chief of Staff, a little bustling man who was such a contrast to the gray-coated officers of the Russian army. A certain kind of intelligence about his new world had come to him. He had been taught to salute all officers, and he had done so in Petrograd until his arm was tired. He knew how to jump out to the edge of a sidewalk, click his heels together, and stand with his right hand trembling with rigidity at his cap. He knew the Russian officer was a good-natured, kindly man, but Maxim was no fool and if anything about could dispel the atmosphere of the grim business of war, it was the late hour of some of the officers' breakfasts, the sleepy eyes of mid-morning, and the way in which there traveled about among the men the reputation of some special officer who furnished a contrast.

For instance, there was Kalpaschnikov, commanding the First Siberian.[8] Maxim did not know it, but Kalpaschnikov, who was in the diplomatic service and once was second secretary in the Washington Embassy, left the Foreign Office service to fight. The First Siberian is a regiment which has already enrolled 20,000 men. This means that it has been wiped out nearly five times! Even Maxim could distinguish between officers and officers. He knew that most of them were good fellows, but not quite "on their toes."

And finally, after the days in Mogilev, came the order to go to the fighting front, somewhere in the south. So the regiment of Maxim marched away in the blinding snowstorm of early winter. There was a railroad journey again and a long march with the astrakhan caps pulled down over the ear tips. Everything was awhirl with snow. "Remember," said the voice of the man who marched next to Maxim. "No German prisoners." "Such are the orders?" "Fool!" said the man on the other side. "Fool! There are no orders.

---

7 General Mikhail Alekseyev (1857–1918) was the last chief of staff and former commander in chief of the Russian Imperial Army, and then commander in chief under the Provisional Government. After the revolution, he fought against the Bolsheviks and died of heart failure.
8 Colonel Andrei Kalpashnikov had raised enough money in the United States to purchase seventy-two ambulances and eight other vehicles, which were shipped semi-assembled to Petrograd in 1917. He and his vehicles, however, became caught up in the rapidly changing political situation in Russia and he was arrested by the new Bolshevik government and imprisoned for five months; when he was released, he fled the country using false papers.

It is understood. The Germans are killing all Cossacks. It is understood. No German prisoners." "You mean--!" "The bayonet," answered the others conclusively. "Certainly, the bayonet. All the army understands." Maxim did not shudder. He laughed to himself in an ugly fashion.

Later on the two men who had told him not to take any German prisoners were seen by him sharing their rations with the refugees from new villages which had been ordered evacuated and burned by the Russians. Maxim wondered. Several days later, on sentry duty, he saw a child crying by the roadside at dawn and pointing into a ditch. The child's mother was there, and Maxim tried to share his rations with her, but he could not because she was frozen stiff. It was all a dream.

Maxim knew nothing more of his movements or his purposes than his rifle knew. The two miles of the second line of front he knew. He knew the sound of shells that screamed out of Russian masked batteries over the heads of the first line of Russian trenches. He knew the sound of German shrapnel that sang in the biting air in their approach. He knew the way a projectile turned the brown earth up from under the white blanket and befouled half an acre of the night's snowfall.

He knew no complicated military strategy, but when he had climbed to the crest of the ridge he could see a hollow of swamp between rocky ridges: a wide swamp exposed to the sweep of fire from either side and in which, there being only ice water and ledges, no night trenching could go on.

He did not know that the German artillery was in an exposed position on the opposite ridge across the swamp where the fir trees stood out black against the sky. He did not know that if the Russian field pieces had sufficient ammunition they could pound that German position to pieces.

The Russians were drawing up regiment after regiment under cover of night into the first line of trenches. Maxim thought there must be gathered under that cover, and ready to charge across the boggy, half-frozen swamp, all the Russian army! There were endless numbers of men under that cover of the first line of trenches. There were endless numbers of men. At dawn it began. There are endless numbers of men in Russia; they are spent prodigally.

Orders and officers' commands poured the open advance over the cover of trenches and into the swamp. Far away on the frosty air sounded the rattle of German machine guns. They were mowing down the advance. Maxim could see! He saw the running figures of men change from vertical to horizontal positions. The swamp was becoming a slaughter hole. Maxim cared nothing. Suddenly he felt himself superhuman. He felt himself able to run across the swamp and all alone with a handful of rocks, if need be, charge the ridge beyond. And in this too he represented the real Russian soldier. He clutched his gun. His regiment was drawn up ready. He had no fear. He cared nothing.

Nothing was terrible in the sight of lines mowed down. Nothing was terrible in the sound of the roar of artillery or the song of shells or the rat-tat-tat of the "3-liners" or the machine guns on the distant ridge which gave out a noise like that of the stem-winder of a watch. Nothing was terrible but the delay. Maxim was drunk with war.

And at last his regiment poured out into the swamp. From the cover of the trenches and the screen of woods ran the new horde of men. With them ran Maxim - Maxim, the flaxen-haired muzhik, with his straight, powerful body of youth, his alert mind, and his potentiality. He had forgotten to pray. He ran on, firing as his regiment advanced across the open. The ice of the swamp was filled with air holes, and in places springs kept the mud soft. In one of these Maxim tripped and fell. He scrambled to his feet and ran on, shouting with his fellows the Russian charging yell: "Hoorah, hoorah!"

Maxim did not know that with proper ammunition at hand no such wild charge would have been necessary. He did not know that the proper ammunition was lying in the snow somewhere thirty miles south of Archangel. He did not know that the shells had been dumped in the snow by the order of some railroad official, and that the freight cars which had carried them had been taken back to Archangel and reloaded with the imported goods of a Russian merchant in Petrograd. He did not know that the railroad official had received 100 rubles a car for his part in the transaction. He did not know that it was Russians who were killing Russians. He thought the enemy was responsible. Maxim, however, recognized that slaughter was going on. He thought, as he ran, of his fancy that the men were like sheep or young beeves.

The sweep of some machine gun mowing down men like the sweep of a sickle or a scythe included Maxim. He went pitching forward with a half-audible grunt. There was not a moment to think of Vera or his mother or the village or even of Russia. He had given all for Russia.

Some days later the English newspapers which came into Petrograd contained a dispatch describing the repulse of a Russian advance. This dispatch the censor blotted out with a sticky black ink, and over the ink he sprinkled sand so that no one curious to know the truth could remove the ink without scratching off the printing. On that same day a raven lit near a thing in the swamp, a thing which looked like a bundle of rags. There were plenty more of such bundles scattered about, as the raven could see. Maxim was not alone. In death, just as in life, he represented the millions which are Russia.

There are those who will find in the story of Maxim - the story of the Russian peasant who dies on the battlefield - only the tale of a simple man snatched from his home, jammed into military service, not knowing clearly why he is preparing to fight, deluded by the governing classes, hastened to the front, and killed like an animal. I believe that anyone who has been with the Russian army will protest against this view.

The Maxims are not as intelligent as the British soldier who has volunteered among more than three million others to "do his little bit" overseas, but the Maxim who lies in the swamp - one dead Russian private from the stupendous number of dead and live Russian privates, one among the inexhaustible, terrifying hordes of fighting men who come at the call of Russia - did not die like an animal. He died like a man.

Maxim on his way from the village to the frost of the swamp learned much of that which to him became a great and living truth - Russia belonged to him, and he belonged to Russia. Holy Russia! This is how Maxim spoke of his country. Compared to Holy Russia, Maxim believed himself so unimportant that in war nothing of him except the service he could render to a common cause was worthy a thought. It was a remarkable and an inspiring thing to find that the Russian soldier who is more a conscripted, herded, government driven soldier than any in war, is serving with all the strength of his free will, with fierce bravery, with self- effacement. Maxim may have been a fool; but fool that he may have been from some points of view, Maxim's soul, if it had its way, would resurrect the body from the swamp where it lies, to serve again in the name of Holy Russia. Vera and Maxim's aged parents may be fools; but fools that they may be, they do not love Russia less because Maxim lies in the swamp where the ravens call; they love Russia more. Maxim for the new Russia has done his part.

Chapter 4

THE BLIGHT

From the Russian army I turned aside to the still more terrible picture of the homeless hordes of the noncombatants. That which I saw of these homeless hordes is more terrible because while the Russian soldier gives all for Russia it appears that the Russian refugee has all taken away.

I awoke one morning in a little town in the middle of western Russia to the realization that I had tossed about, disturbed in sleep by voices which, in the gray dawn, had mumbled along under my window. Like the flow of a stream, the voices were going by in the narrow street below, and at first I thought they were the voices of new Russian regiments swinging onward toward the front again with the rhythmic marching swing of the Czar's armies. But it was a stranger and even more tragic procession upon which I looked.

During the night snow had fallen upon the streets and upon the two-storied pink, gray, green, and pale-blue plastered shops and houses of the place. With their uncertain, plodding, stumbling feet causing this dry snow to creak beneath, a straggling irregular procession of children, women, and men moved onward in the gray of breaking morning. Some walked straight, bearing parcels and sacks in their hands; others were bent by the burdens of their possessions, or by mere weariness, or as if the eternal cold had broken the spirit. The heads of all, even of the young children, were set doggedly. All talked or shouted or whined, but none save one of all the hundreds turned to look behind, and so it appeared that the mind of each ragged creature was traveling a little faster than the body toward an unknown goal. The one who looked backward was an old man, and because, while he remained within sight, he stopped, turned, stared at the night which was retreating over the western horizon, gazed far away wistfully, and shook his head as if he could not understand, I thought that he was a sadder sight than all the rest and perhaps more to be pitied. He could not forget the years he had lived nor his home. Foolish Russian: all that made life for him had been wiped out, and it was evident that he still hoped that this fact by strange magic would disappear into the haze of dreams!

He and his fellows, plunging onward, half fed, half starved, half clothed, and half frozen, had come, no doubt, from a village near the front which the Russian officers had ordered evacuated and burned for "military necessity." They were refugees.

In Russia when one speaks of refugees, one does not mean, as one might in other belligerent countries, those who, for safety's sake only, have moved away from danger; one means men or women or children who have fled from the scorch of war as countless animals and insects fly before the approach of fire in grass or timber. In Russia "refugee" usually means one who has had all past association permanently rubbed out as one rubs writing from a blackboard; the Russian refugee usually has lost village, home, animals, personal belongings, and often all friends, relatives, and even sense of the points of the compass. In front of him is the vast Russian plain and the future; behind him is the lost past. Life, constructed year after year; the cup from which he drank, the room in which his grandfather died, and even the view from the back door have been wiped away now. Life is erased. Dazed, frost-bitten, sick, footsore, a human being stripped of most of the distinctions which had separated him from his cow or his pig, clinging now to existence as his most precious possession, herding with others, as sheep in a storm, or broken off from the herd as a lame animal falls behind: on and on he goes. Where? God knows.

I asked a member of one of the war committees in Moscow how many refugees were in Russia. He said: "Fourteen million." A Government official told me: "Probably eleven million." I said: "I do not believe that we realize this thing; in the United States." The Russian artillery officer at Vitebsk to whom I spoke then replied: "Nor do we. But it has been exaggerated. There are not over eight or nine million refugees." Eight or nine million! His low estimate was more than the total population of Canada! After a time I asked: "Where do they go?" He said: "Ah, about such a thing who can tell? There is nothing so sad. I have seen with my own eyes a woman whose journey over the fields and roads had been interrupted by childbirth. She had to stop. They were both frozen."

In Petrograd there are a million new residents, and many of these are refugees who have stood the long journey from Poland or elsewhere on the war front. In Moscow the number is over a million. Thus the population of these two cities alone has been swelled by a number of persons larger than the entire population of Maine, New Hampshire, Vermont, and Rhode Island; this is the contribution that war has made to the two cities, and in the main it is a contribution of individuals whose lives have been uprooted, whose pasts are obliterated, and whose futures are as blank as unprinted pages. "What will be their destiny?" I asked of one of the editors best known in Russia. He said: "I fear that Destiny has too much just now in her head to make any plans for these migrating millions. The sparrow's fall of the past has assumed great significance as compared to the fate of one of these."

Nowhere could I receive any clear answer to the question of what was to become of all this homeless horde. I went to Vladislas Zukowski, perhaps the most prominent man in the public affairs of the Poland of yesterday, and considered the Polish leader in the Third Duma. He shook his head. "I can only speak for Poland," he said. "The number of Polish refugees in Russia, as distinguished from the other refugees, probably is nearly a million and a half. The Russian Government contributes five or six millions of rubles every month for their maintenance and about ten millions of rubles have been spent on their clothing. But – " He paused and we both understood that six million rubles a month meant an expenditure of a little over a dollar per refugee. "In August and September, and even later, no relief action had been organized," he went on. "Thousands upon thousands of children were lost or perished from exposure and exhaustion, all over the fields and roads of western Russia. The land is loaded with unidentified burials. Polish national institutions have centered their efforts of relief today in the Congress of Polish Institutions in Moscow. The Russian Government regarded the relief action favorably and granted large credits. Many of our refugees are secure from starvation.

"It is not only the peasant who has suffered; understand that the land owners and professional classes have also lost everything. No compensation is in sight. Sometimes the army authorities can act quickly to protect those who have lost everything by army service, but the civil authorities will have to delay indefinitely relief to ruined land owners and those in the professions. Owing to the uncertainty of what is to become of them, the refugee Poles in Russia, whether peasants or not, are in terrible bitterness. Moral depression is evident. There is nothing to live for.

"Perhaps this depression could be relieved materially by sympathy from the western nations. But remember that such expressions of sympathy must not be of the kind to irritate Russian opinion, for that would be fatal. Remember, too, that after the Russian army retired from Poland the Polish question was no longer an internal question of the Russian Empire; it is now an international question."[1]

---

1 Child is referring to the question of Polish autonomy and self-determination. Poland was carved out of existence through the Three Partitions by Russia, Prussia, and Austria at the end of the eighteenth century. As World War One destroyed old boundaries and threatened to cause the collapse of several major empires, the creation of a reconstituted Poland seemed possible.

The real truth is that Russia herself cannot conceive the magnitude of the horde homeless staggering out of the West, wandering in Russian fields and roads, fleeing this way and that without plan or purpose, dazed by war: old men and women and children driven eastward across the great plain, as insects scurry out of fields aflame, and in their countless numbers making ridiculous the importance of the human individual.

With refugees, educated and uneducated, Polish and Russian, Jew and Gentile, young and old, directly when I could, through an interpreter when I could not, I talked. The similarity of their stories produced a strange effect. The repetition time after time of a series of events by which war and fate had caught each one by the throat, torn each away from life and left him little but dawn and dusk, pain and chaos and the dull remnants of this sense of self-preservation, produced a feeling that destiny had a like fate in store for us all. It was hard to realize that my people in the United States were busy distinguishing between good cooking and bad, between becoming clothes and those clothes which are unbecoming, between mattresses of felt and those of hair.

Why, here in Russia, seven, eight, ten million people had stumbled forward, all going at life blindly, and some were dropping into roadside ditches morning, noon, and night. Always the story was the same, and so at last there looms up a great picture of the refugee hordes. War is afar. News comes of battles and the changing fortunes of the conflict on the great Russian front. Day after day troops pour by out of Russia's great reserve of men toward the conflagration of war. And then, little by little, war creeps toward the village or the town. Those who live in the houses stand at their doorways at dusk to see wagons and motor trucks laden with wounded rumble away toward railroads and hospitals set up in the rear of the army. The fighting front is writhing like a snake, they say. Soldiers limping back from field hospitals tell of the gains or losses and of the terrible spray of metal from concentrated German artillery fire. War is coming toward the village! The people instinctively look toward the west waiting for war to lift its head over the horizon, to come flowing like molten metal through the groves of trees beyond the town. "There was something childish about that," said a refugee doctor to me. "All our people kept looking and looking." I thought of the way children stand on a curb listening for the first strains of the band and watching for the first flecks of color of the circus parade. But here in these villages the people, lifting their noses to the faint breeze from the setting sun, could smell war. War was coming.

At night, miles away, there were red flushes in the sky! It was always the same. People, frightened, began to send their valuables to friends in cities. Rumors poured into the villages. Soldiers, Red Cross nurses, refugees from farther west came hurrying through, bearing endless, conflicting stories from which no conclusion could be reached. War might swallow the town, and it might not. "Those who flee show their folly," said the keeper of the meat shop.

But the Russian priest in his long, black, threadbare robe shook his head. Some of the landed proprietors had gone; they had money enough to reach the railroad and Kiev; others of them able to go still remained, doubtless because it was incredible that destruction could come and in one swoop wipe out the pictures of a lifetime. The sound of the guns was so far away; rarely were they heard. There were miles and miles between the village and the unbelievable. And, as for the peasants, the able-bodied men left were not many and women and children could not be expected to rise from the supper table and fly headlong across the stubble fields into the Russian winter. The moment had not come. And so the life of the village went on.

It went on until there came a daybreak which brought the sound of cavalry in the village streets. A dozen Cossacks escorting one of their officers had ridden out of the night, and in front of the telegraph station they sat astride their horses in slouching attitudes suggestive of lack of sleep. Not long after their arrival an officer in infantry sent four men out with posters to plaster against the walls and posts. The order had come. The village was to be evacuated!

When the chatter over this order was at its height a crackling sound was heard, and anyone who looked up at the mansion of the richest man in all the town could see smoke bellying out of its open doors and flames licking through its roof and igniting the oily tops of evergreens which overspread it. It was the first. In substance the story was always the same. In advance there is destruction, but in no advance is there destruction such as that which goes on in retreat. Therefore the village which might become for the Germans a haven and a resting place in which some vestige of shelter or remnants of food might be found must be turned into a coal-black waste of smoking ruins hissing beneath the fall of the cold rain of early winter. The time had come for flight. Sometimes the notice was given days beforehand; sometimes there was no notice but that of red-eyed, blue-mouthed soldiers marching in a broken burlesque of the wonderful Russian march rhythm, dragging field pieces through the mud in retreat. And sometimes whole towns must be on the move before nightfall fleeing toward - Nowhere.

In flight there develops the communal spirit. I have seen refugees come out of the fields and off the roadsides west of a Russian railroad town in groups of fives and tens. Though these groups had tramped and ridden from evacuated places far apart, and had never seen each other before, they were all possessed of the one idea of reaching together a main thoroughfare. This idea bound group to group until the station was so crowded with wandering humanity, the floor so covered with the prostrate bodies of old men and children sleeping off their exhaustion, but sticking together as if mere numbers had virtues of salvation, and the general accumulation so great the railroad was folced to furnish box cars to move the soggy crowd onward again.

For it is the madness of the refugee to seek the railroad. So it is always: the field to the path, the path to the roadway, the roadway to the thoroughfare, the thoroughfare to the railroad, of which there are so few in Russia, and then on to the city, to the center, to the place - any place - where the rest of living beings have crowded together! The railroad and Moscow, Kiev, and Petrograd are like magnets toward which the refugees, like tiny iron filings, are dragged. They feel within them the answer to some irresistible call of gregariousness. And such has been the movement of the homeless millions.

The number of those who have died on the way will never be known. How many unburied corpses are covered by the snow of the great Russian plain cannot be guessed; the thaw of the spring will tell. Their names have gone; they will be forgotten. Thousands will never know whether mothers, fathers, children, brothers, sisters, or wives are dead or merely lost forever.

In Moscow I met a young officer of infantry, an engineer, a graduate of a technical institute in Petrograd. He wanted to talk to me in German, but that is forbidden in Russia, and even English may not be used over the telephone systems of the capitals. Therefore we fell into inadequate French, as we stood together after nightfall before a lighted shop window. A young girl in shabby clothing came out of the shadows and talked to the officer in a hoarse whisper, glancing about furtively like a frightened animal ready to flee to any cover. He turned to me. "Refugee," said he laconically but with a note of tenderness in his voice. He gave her a paper ruble and motioned to her to go away. "Refugee. She will never see her family again. There are endless numbers of girls who have nothing to live for. The war drives the herds of mankind into the cities."

He shrugged his shoulders. "It is too cold to stand here longer," he said after a moment. I remembered his conversation when I saw half a hundred young women just outside the Warsaw station in the empire's capital shivering in their shawl and rags, and shoes so worn by endless steps over the frozen ruts of the roads that many pairs were bound together with strings and windings of twisted cloth. The stream of driven humanity which eddies around the metropolitan railroad terminals, in spite of all efforts of the Government to shut off the unwelcome flood, is made up of great numbers of young women and almost no young men. There are old men, infirm or aged women, and endless children who still laugh, chatter, and fall asleep like young tired kittens or puppies wherever a bit of warmth causes drowsiness, without realization of the calamity behind them and the chaos of life into which they fare forward. But it is the young women who stare ahead so blankly out of their frightened brown and blue eyes. The others, thoughtless, dull with age or ignorant in youth, find the drama of the day in a plate of soup or a scrap of rag to wind about a cold red wrist; it is only the young women who seem to sense the menace of tomorrows.

The cities themselves are dazed by the situation; the accumulations of hordes coming from somewhere and going nowhere is frightful. These people cannot be allowed to die; there would be difficulty in finding means to bury them all! And so the dazed and frightened composite face of the refugee stares into the dazed, frightened face of the city and each challenges the other for an answer.

Into the gullets of the cities pours the flood, and the cities cannot digest and assimilate it. I counted 600 refugees coming in dripping with melting snow through the gate of a soup kitchen in Petrograd; surely not over 100 were capable of any productive labor. It was a crowd of dependents. They were a selected lot because they were the individuals who had reached the end of their pilgrimage by hook or crook. They had started for Petrograd and, while others had fallen on roadsides or interned themselves in hospitals or wayside relief stations or been considerate enough to die on the mad journey, these had arrived. But even these constituted a mob without a leaven of hope.

"They are mostly agricultural people," said the bureaucrat who deals with the committees of relief. "Children, useless old men, a few women of maturity and young women who can-not read or write. At the best, not one in four can be said to be self-supporting, and the 25 per cent who are capable of labor have no education for labor in cities. Nor have the Russian cities any vast labor market to absorb their terrible numbers. Do you know what General says? He says it would be a great mercy to set up a guillotine at all the railroad stations; that the guillotine would save so much suffering to the millions of the lost and to Russia."

In a crude way the cities try to keep together the refugee's body and his soul. Great barracks have been built of wood. Warehouses have been opened. I went to one of these hopeless hotels. There one can see straw laid along the two long walls with a walking space between, and hurrying down this dimly lit pathway, with hundreds of human beings from anywhere stretched out upon the straw, one can find that memories of cattle shows and exhibits of livestock come back to the mind so vividly that it is hard to realize that these odors rise from humanity. That terrible infections have not been sweeping along with these herds of mankind is something to make one gasp; that epidemics may not come down upon the homeless hordes is the subject for a thoughtful Russian prayer.

No one knows how the hundreds of thousands are fed. Not all the feeding stations which have been established can take care of the demands of the mouths. The hunger of the refugees is like the hunger of young birds helpless in the nest with mouths agape creating nothing and ready to consume anything, and this hunger has the usual animal insistence that to be fed is the trade made with nature when one consents to go on living. In exactly this spirit the refugees take that which is given them. Their insistence to be fed is inspiriting because it measures the strength of purpose of mankind to live. That they are able to complain that they have not had enough or that the food which they have is not good is a pleasant fact to observe because it indicates that humanity, even in the last ditch, eternally cries out for better and for more.

I was watching a group of soldiers between Mogilev and the fighting front sharing their rations with a half-starved group of refugees. The dirty, frost-cracked hand of an old, bent man rose in the air holding a piece of white bread aloft, and from beneath this bread the old man roared his execrations to the skies. "The Russian soldier is a good fellow," said I to the officer who sat beside me in the army motor car. "Apparently he is always willing to share his food with these wanderers driven out of the burned-over country." "Yes. And stand ingratitude like that of the old man who is whining because the bread is not black," said the other. "But who cares? The loss of everything is enough to spoil one's temper."

And yet in that group which, having fed, trudged on in pairs or in single file toward nowhere, there was more than the mere living up to the obligation not to die. There was something of the picturesque. Three of the young women whose cheeks were pink in the cold wore their hair in peculiar braids bound about their necks so that the hair would serve to keep out the fine, dry snow which the icy wind blew across the Russian plain. The children, whose short, tired legs dragged on, were clad in materials of many colors, and one wore a meal sack through which armholes had been cut and beneath which a stuffing of straw made the slender body appear to be the body of a gnome. Privation has aged the faces of the children, but still they laugh as they go. The older figures bend forward. Women too old to leave the hearthside trudge along toward uncertain night falls, and men, who have lived long years and accumulated a maze of wrinkles upon patient peasant faces under and near a single thatched roof in Galicia or Poland, now lift their rope-bound feet mechanically, one after the other, because suddenly fate has said that there is no one spot in which they may stay.

The typical refugee band was picturesque because it was clad in many colors and many strange and ragged draperies; And it was a band, not only of tragedy, but also of romance, because it was more itinerant than the gypsies and its end was more unreal and mythical and mysterious than the pot of gold behind the rainbow.

It is difficult to read the thoughts behind the peasant faces. "They are expressionless as platters," said a Russian Red Cross nurse. "They must have been contorted when war crept upon them and drove them from their little world. But now all emotion is worn out." So it is! I have watched them enter feeding stations with countenance after countenance of the hundreds as bare of meaning as the bottoms of so many milk pails. Peasants and occasional former shopkeepers and artisans alike show the same look of dulled sensibilities. There are almost no flashes of joy, of grief, of hope, of self; there are hunger, weariness, and the other expressions of animals. Sometimes in the crowds, undistinguished by clothes or cleanliness, will appear one figure whose bearing and whose eyes show a different state of mind. To one of these I asked an interpreter to speak. "I was a doctor," said the lonely man. "I had the position of the well-loved physician in a group of towns. I owned several houses and I lived well. I had been to Berlin and to London. But the army swept back upon us in the retreat from Warsaw. Finally, all went and left burning baggage wagons close to the wooden houses. A great wind blew, and the fire swept all away. My own roof was higher than any, and from it the flames jumped into the woodland. All night long as we ran away the sky was red. The people were driving pigs and cattle before them and pushing carts piled high with their belongings over the fields. None wished to go too far because they dreamed that they could go back after a time and build up their homes again. The sky was red, and I could see the faces of my old friends. At the end of two days there were twenty-five of us in one lot and there was nothing to eat. An old man died under the full sun. There was not a tree or a shelter standing anywhere. We could hear artillery far away, and then as far as we could see everything had been burned - fields, woods, fences, houses, all the grass. There was no food for the animals and so they were abandoned. All the world was charred black and dusted over with gray ashes. Sometimes we found a horse which had foundered."

The interpreter asked him other questions. He said that he had a wife. He had left her at a refugee camp while he had gone out to find food and water. "But when I came back soldiers had driven all before them. I have never seen her since. There were no telegraphs, no trains, no news. The world was blank. She had gone. Days later I found a little girl of five in the woods. She had been with us. But she could tell me nothing. I began to forget all I knew of my profession. I can do nothing or very little now. All is strange. And here is where I must feed -there is no other way to keep life in my body." He reached for his bowl of soup and stared at the steam which arose from it as if the vapors were those ascending around an oracle which might speak of the future.

"The peasants suffer most in body," said the Russian nurse smoothing her starched white headdress. "But the educated persons used to luxury suffer more in the mind. I have heard of the suffering in Belgium, but there, at least, is shelter and familiar surroundings. Here in Russia refugees have been driven hundreds of miles from a land which few will ever see again. Men who were rich - landowners, teachers, and professional men and their wives and children - are like beggars of the gutter." "What will become of them? No one can say," replied an official of the Department of the Interior. "We have tried to arrange colonies in Siberia. The Siberian members of the Duma opposed us. Some of those who acted as if they were representatives of the refugees opposed us. Some money has been appropriated for relief. Then the Jews - whatever one may think of them in Russia - have done wonderful things to help their own kind. We want to keep the refugees out of the cities. We ought to be shipping carloads to Siberia. That would be wisest."

One evening I went to supper with a Russian family in Petrograd. The other guests - more than two dozen in number - were grave old men and healthy young women. Some played violin, cello, and piano, while others chatted in corners. There were music and some low singing, and after a time nearly all joined in Polish dances, whirling this way and that and emphasizing the rhythm of the music by stamping the feet. Under the light from the chandelier in the high ceiling it was possible to see, for the first time, that of all these Polish guests, so well poised in manner, so equipped to converse entertainingly of world-wide affairs and so plainly accustomed to luxury, the clothing was shabby. All wore an air of poverty.

"My friends are all refugees from Poland," said the hostess. "Refugees!" "That stout old man over there was one of the large landholders," she said. "He now has nothing. Landholding is a business in itself. He has no training for anything else. What can he do? Well, you see, his life is ended."

"There is a young girl with the mass of golden hair," she went on. "She has lost all the members of her family. She was engaged to a young officer. He was shot. She came to Petrograd without so much as an extra handkerchief. She has been here for months and has not seen any one she ever saw before, or heard news from any one she ever knew. And yet she can laugh."

"The bearded gentleman who joins in none of this merrymaking is a professor from Warsaw. His name is ---. He always appears to be deep in thought. He is a learned man, but he cannot understand. Some think he is going mad, but that is absurd. He is reflecting. It is so hard to have one's country destroyed and life blown away as if it were a fine powder to disappear in one puff of war. Oh, Moscow and Petrograd are full of such refugees with their brooding minds."

The peasants with their platter faces sometimes show flashes of realization. Perhaps no peasants are as meditative as the Russians; among them are many illiterate philosophers. One of these sat on the stone curbing near the Warsaw station staring into the gutter or dully watching the new regiments of tan-coated soldiers who were drilling in the square under a blinding snowstorm. "You see there is a man who cannot be a soldier," said the army doctor who was with us. "He is knotted by rheumatism. There is a man who has suffered pain, I tell you." "Don't sit there," he said in Russian. "Why not?" asked the refugee, caressing his bandaged legs with his flannel-swathed hands. "The snow is cool." He spoke again, leering at the doctor with one eye closed. "What does he say?" I asked. "He says there is no past - there is no future," the doctor told me. "He says that, when there is neither, it is wise to remain seated."

But in spite of all the misery of the great, homeless hordes of Russia, the number and woe of which have never been equaled, and in spite of the fact that life is rubbed out behind them and that they stare toward Nowhere, the hundreds one can see suffuse a kind of glow. I think it is the glow of the human instinct to keep on.

Thousands of square miles are empty and blackened by the scorch of war; over the charred country lies an unbroken blanket of snow. More persons than live in the whole of Canada are driven haphazard over the Russian plain or into the overloaded cities. Some, half mad, have forgotten their names. These millions are almost like animals pursued, herded, driven, desperate. But not quite. The millions - the seven, the ten, the fourteen millions, whatever one may guess - are still suffusing a glow which animals could not. It is the glow of human instinct to press on toward intelligent and eternal purposes. The horse, the cow, and the pig lie down and die on the Russian roadway. It is only the refugee who reaches the cities. The refugee is often nearly an animal, but never quite an animal; the refugee stripped of all else still carries with him the human will.

In the story of the Russian refugee there are those who, from a distance, will find only a tale of suffering, of wasted lives, of menacing future, of unspeakable destruction, of bodies wracked, hearts embittered, heads made stupid with woe, and spirits crushed. But I believe that those who, knowing this story at first hand, are able to keep their intelligence from being drowned in the torrent of horror, with all their might will assert that the true picture is not so much the picture of the failures of humanity as it is the picture of the triumph of humanity. For every refugee who acts in the Russian drama of the homeless hordes there are dozens of human beings with a reawakened spirit of the brotherhood of man who are building for us new faith that a human being is not merely so many pounds of meat filled with nerves, whose greatest achievement is not producing for his own comfort steam-heated buildings, fireless cookers, patent razors, and a style of millinery, and whose destiny does not end with the snuffing out of the spark of mortal life.

I saw that war had brought a blight more fearful than imagination could conceive; but I cannot forget the communal spirit of the refugees among themselves. I saw men who shivered at the door of soup stations in Petrograd give up their brass soup checks to women in a herd of women who had just come in from their long march. I saw a lone, footsore Jewish refugee overtake a blonde-haired man and woman who walked with their heads cast down, observing which he greeted them and to encourage these strangers began to sing and dance - a grotesque imitation of Puck in a benevolent mood. I saw Little Russians at a mid-Russia railway station wake their own children from sleep on benches so that there might be space for the children of others to have their short measure of sleep. I saw tired men pick up the children of strangers and carry them onward as if they had been their own. At a time when self-preservation appeared to be the only instinct left, suddenly it seemed that social consciousness rose to its height and the common good of all overtopped the sense of individual welfare.

Nor can I forget that the plight of the refugees after all is not as vivid in the memory as the incidents of human sympathy. Russian soldiers poked fun at the grotesque appearance of the wanderers, but they gave to the hungry their own rations. The very men who are said to be brutalized by war, played with children and built fires for the women. I met a Cossack who carried behind him on his horse an aged Jew, and I thought that this was a strange symbol, but later all the information I could gather tended to show, contrary to the tales which are told in America, that along the front the war has not sharpened the anti-Jewish feeling except where German sympathizers have excited it, but, on the contrary, has tended to wipe out prejudice at a time when it is less noticeable that a man is a Jew or a Russian, than that he is a human being.

I saw a nation of people turning from interest in self to interest in the common good of all. One of the many professional beggars of the streets said to my interpreter, "My business is ruined by the war. Before a man or woman arrives at the spot where I sit they have had dozens of tin boxes thrust under their noses - relief, lazarets, the refugees, the widows, always relief - tag days, subscriptions, tin boxes! Very well - I am content."

The refugees suffer. But the refugees learn to know the spirit which lies deep down within them. And the refugees are only a fraction of the people of Russia. The rest of the Russian people because of the refugees are learning to know themselves. They are sensing the revival of social consciousness, they are acting the prologue before a new era of recognition of a spiritual life.

Chapter 5

CZAR AND PEOPLE

Russia and her people, achieving a new step toward progress in the midst of a seethe of war, cannot be understood without knowing Russia and her government and her people as they are today. Of the surprises to be found in the Empire, none is so great as that of the realization of misconceptions of Russia existing outside her borders, and especially in the United States.

When I came out of Russia, Englishmen and Americans flung at me six questions, and I found that by answering these questions which in the main concerned that which may be called news interest, I had sketched Russia as she is today, her Czar, her government, her people, and her awakening spirit. These were the six questions: Why did the Czar supplant the Grand Duke? Will Russia make a separate peace? Is the German influence strong? Will there be a revolution? Has the Russian army sufficient ammunition and supplies? Is Russia permeated by graft?

These were inevitable questions. They were asked of me by those who know that I have had opportunities to observe Russia in her trying moments, and that through official channels and a visit as a guest of the Russian General Staff, and as a wanderer in and out of Moscow and Petrograd, I would be able to tell something of Russia from behind the scenes. The answers to them involve much that is more significant and interesting than life in the trenches at an inactive winter front or salvos of artillery shot off to amuse and educate the rare American visitor.

Russia is an empire of contradictions. The difficulty with anything that is said about Russia is that at once it must be qualified. For instance, "The Russian people are suppressed; Russia is an autocracy." It is true. But behold the apparent contradiction: nowhere more than in Russia is developed, in men or women, the sense of being individual; nowhere, certainly not in the United States, is there such a democracy of human feeling. Again: "Russia is a country of peasants; three-fourths of the Russians are agricultural people, who live scattered over vast areas." But Russia is not a country of peasants in the sense that the peasants of Russia are expressed in the Russia which we know. They are not expressed; it is the bureaucracy and the universities and the cities which are expressed. Again: "The Russian is a person without morals." But the real Russian - the Russian of the millions - is a person of wonderful sweetness of soul and knows how to live skillfully, even under difficulties, a simple, pure, and gentle life.

Not only is Russia a country of contradictions, but, because it has long suffered from poverty of information and prohibition against free statement of fact and expression of opinion, it is a country of mystery. A pall of darkness hangs over Russia still, and it is the darkness which gathers where education is not and where vast numbers of men are governed, watched, and disciplined by the few. This darkness is not so black as it has been smudged, and it is thinning, but it creates apprehensions of menaces which have no real existence, and it creates rumors. Russia is a country of contradictions and rumors. Perhaps it is because of this fact that almost all of the questions currently asked about Russia must be answered in a way to surprise the questioner.

When I went to Russia, I myself, because there was so much misinformation about Russia outside her borders, wanted to know why the Czar had taken command of the army at the front and supplanted the Grand Duke Nicholas.[1] For that and other reasons I tried to have the opportunity of talking with the Czar. I had pointed out to the Russians and their English allies that the Czar would gain and not lose if his human and real personality were better known to his people just now, and that in no way could conviction be carried better to them than by way of America. To have a faithful picture of the Czar appear in the United States would help in creating greater friendly interest between the United States and Russia. More than that, an outside publication, reprinted widely in Russia, would reach truly the Russian people, whereas any Russian-made word picture of the Czar would be regarded in the same light as the idealized conventional portrait of a red-uniformed, beautiful, and benign Little Father which hangs in every public hall in Russia. The plans for a sudden drive on the southern battle front, made in great secrecy, with movement of troops by night and days of closed telegraph and mail service to the outside world, put an end to my expectations. But in my attempt I had come into close contact with ministers and staff officers who constantly are close to the Czar's personality and to the peculiar atmosphere which surrounds him. I had heard already from some of those party leaders in the Duma who, at longer range, discern little in Nicholas II which is inspiring, or indeed which is not menacing to the growth of liberalism and

---

1 In the summer of 1915, Nicholas II decided to replace his cousin, Grand Duke Nicholas Nikolaevich as Supreme Commander of the Russian Imperial Army after a series of military failures.

to the place of the Duma as a fact rather than, as at present, a form of true legislative assembly.

The Czar is a zealot. He is intense. He is religious to the point of superstition. He believes firmly enough that the destiny of a hundred and seventy million persons and their posterity is in his charge. Whatever may be the narrowness of his view, there can be no doubt about his sincerity in wishing to maintain the Russian dynasty as nearly as possible in the state in which it was when he inherited it from his father. He loves his people; if he believes that democratic government is dangerous for Russia, it is because he believes that it is dangerous to stability and not merely that he feels that it menaces the prerogative of the monarchy. To him the dynasty is an heirloom; it must be handed down to the czarevitch as it now stands, not because it is a good thing for a line of emperors, but because he believes it a good thing for the millions of people. The Czar may not be a man of such imagination, but he is a man of much sentiment.

He is small. His full-length photograph at a quick glance might be taken for a somewhat retouched portrait of King George of England, with some of the lines of character effaced.[2] "He has a gravity which is out of keeping with his short stature and with a certain lack of forcefulness," said a foreign diplomat. "Being the Czar is a serious business to him." It is doubly serious now. But occasionally he is quite ready to unbend. For instance, he often jumps out of his motor car to sit among groups of his soldiers, and has allowed photographs to be taken of him in the informal moments. It was suggested to him that the publication of these pictures would be excellent to show the Russian people that the Czar was human and lovable. He laughed and said: "Perhaps so, but I would feel that it was making a great booby of me."

The Emperor talks English excellently; indeed, this is the language which is most often used in the royal family group. This group in Petrograd and in the great Winter Palace is surrounded by wall after wall of isolation from the people; the Czarina and the four daughters, Olga, Tatiana, Marie, and Anastasia, take some interest in charities, but otherwise are real to the Russian people only through their photographs. The war, however, has increased the opportunities for their work and has done something to make them more like living beings. For instance, when the report arose that the Czar had offered his eldest daughter, Olga, to the Prince of Rumania in exchange for Rumania's entering the war on the side of the Allies, those Russians who spoke to me about it were inclined to forget the position of Olga

---

2 The two monarchs were, in fact, first cousins – their mothers were sisters – and it was often noted how much they resembled one another.

as a marriageable member of royalty and to comment upon her as a young girl with all the thoughts and feelings which a young girl well might have under the circumstances.

That the family of the Czar suffers from the circulation of cruel, despicable rumors, there can be no doubt. The system by which the Czar and his family are made unreal by isolation is, of course, also a system which results in clouding the truth in a fog of myths, whispered all about and in these days of war traveling hither and thither with more activity than ever. The printed word may be censored in Russia and is censored rigidly, but the spoken word travels fast enough and is soon distorted; during wars it travels like wildfire by the soldiers who go and come, from and to, their homes in distant corners of the empire.

So it is that the court of the Czar is pictured as an institution of the Middle Ages, a court in which intrigue and conspiracy always move. There is a definite court party which shows itself in politics and always upon the side of reaction. There is the Black Hundred.[3] There is Princess Ignatiaovna,[4] whose brilliant salons are said to originate many a delicate plan. A member of an imperial ballet, through her relationship with a noble of the inner circle, is said to determine contracts for munitions. There are stories that the Empress Dowager Marie, mother of the Czar, is not pleased that the czarevitch, now in his twelfth year, has passed safely through a childhood of delicate health and is still in existence, and that the reason for this is that she would prefer a different line of succession. The story is circulated that this young Alexis is suffering from tuberculosis: that he is a hopeless weakling. This story and others like it are refuted by the appearance of the heir apparent himself, who, with his father, goes among the troops. He plays hard and is a great favorite among the big-hearted Russian soldiers around the so-called palace at Mogilev, the

---

3 The name "Black Hundreds" refers to a number of anti-revolutionary groups, all of them ultra-conservative, ultra-nationalist, and anti-Semitic. Most of these groups were founded in the wake of the 1905 Revolution and had the support and, occasionally, the financial backing of the government in fighting the rise tide of revolution from 1905 to 1917.

4 Child may be referring to Vera Ignatievna Gedroits (1870-1932), a woman with a fascinating story. Gedroits was a medical doctor, the first woman professor of surgery, the first woman military surgeon in Russia, and the first woman to serve as a physician to the Imperial Court of Russia. She lived openly as a lesbian, dressing in traditionally male clothing, but also entered into a marriage of convenience to facilitate her leaving Russia to study medicine in Switzerland. She also wrote poetry and, after returning to Russia, she helped to found a journal and tried to surround herself with literary acquaintances.

general staff headquarters of the Czar, and at places nearer the trenches. "A fine boy!" said privates to me with enthusiasm.[5]

But, nonetheless, the court of the Czar, whether or not the whispered stories are false or true, is a court painted by gossips as medieval, and around it are woven stories of strange and sinister machinations. No one of good sense finds much in these stories to believe, but there is one personality whose presence at court tends to give credence to almost any rumor. He has brought into the regime of the dynasty a flavor of centuries gone. It is difficult to believe that such a person could exist in such a place in the year 1916.

Have you ever heard of Rasputin? Rasputin was a hermit priest in Siberia. No one can say exactly by what steps or plans or devices he came to Petrograd. First he was a hermit priest in Siberia, a person affecting mysticism, and then suddenly he became the most extraordinary figure in the empire. Conversation about him is conducted in hushed voices and he is credited with a vast and menacing power. From a little cottage he jumped into the midst of the Czar's family. He was like a giant appearing out of a bottle. Someone had rubbed a magic lamp.

Perhaps members of the Czar's household can explain the story of Rasputin. No one else knows. Some say he was the creature of an intriguing circle of courtiers who "planted" Rasputin in the Winter Palace; others tell the questioner that Rasputin is supposed to have had magic curative powers by which the life or health of the young czarevitch was preserved. His function was uncertain. He may have acted as spiritual adviser to the Czar or the Czarina; he may have acted as a doctor applying mystic boons; he may have been the tool of intrigue, or he may have been one of those rare, dark, rough individuals who in the history of monarchies have been able to worm themselves into the very household of the sovereign. In any case, his is the strangest figure in the world. Almost illiterate, he was a power in Russia.

Huge in stature and countenance, with massive features which were capable of expressing a kindliness or a giant's passions, Rasputin was a rather unclean and greasy person who dressed by preference in a slovenly hermit's robe, over the collar of which hung the dark hair of his enormous leonine head and down the front of which fell his priest's beard. He was under forty. "And yet he had an air of extraordinary magnetism," said one who came into contact with him.

Not long ago a young peasant girl, claiming that Rasputin had done her a great wrong, stuck a knife into him. No one who had heard of Rasputin was surprised; whatever may have been his holiness of spirit, far and wide and

---

5 The young heir had hemophilia.

even among cultured Russians he was considered to be a dangerous profligate. "But no one came forward to present the evidence," I was told. "Rasputin has great power - woe betide the person who calls down his hatred! Only one person has dared to tweak the nose of this man. That was the Grand Duke Nicholas. When Rasputin insisted upon visiting the fighting front, the grand duke sent word that it would be easier for Rasputin to go down than to go back. So the priest stayed away. That was characteristic of the grand duke. He was loved, but he was feared. Even Rasputin feared him."

And so this medieval figure throws its shadow across the court of the Czar, inviting the currency of strange, wild tales, and giving to Russia another broad stripe of the color of mystery and menace. When I left Russia, Rasputin was still living. Later reports came from Russia that he had been slain. Is he alive or dead? Who knows?[6]

No doubt the Czar's perspective is such that he cannot see that such mysteries as the mystery of Rasputin cause the people to forget that the Czar himself is a simple, an earnest, and probably a lovable man. He has his faults; he is capable of small prejudices, and at times (as when he petulantly snubbed Alexander Guchkov,[7] the leader of the Octobrist party and president of the Third Duma, by pretending at a reception that he did not know that Guchkov belonged to the Moscow deputation) he is capable of something less than the kind of statesmanship which might be expected of him. But it is his soldiers who in these days see him as he is. A great intensity of feeling is confined in this Little Father who wants so much to be great of soul and great in action, who is so filled by his religion and by the love of his little boy and by the desire to preserve Russia and make her glorious.

"There is no doubt of his bravery," said a military attaché to me at the officers' mess at the Russian General Staff. "He would go to the first line of trenches and even remain under fire if good counsel were not against it. Of

---

6 Grigorii Rasputin (1872-1916) did indeed become very close to the Romanov royal family because of his ability to calm and easy the suffering of Alexis during his bleeding episodes. As a consequence, Nicholas II and Alexandra became dependent on Rasputin and their trust in him soon extended to other areas, including political matters. This, combined with his influence over and seduction of, many of the noble wives of the capital, made him much reviled, and resulted in his murder by a group of noble men in December 1916. The story of his death – or the supposed difficulty in killing him – is infamous. Child is correct in observing that "the mystery of Rasputin" contributed to a decline in respect for the Russian monarchy.
7 A. I. Guchkov (1862–1936) was a Duma member sent as a representative of the Provisional Government to demand the abdication of Nicholas II. He served as minister of war for a short period in the new Provisional Government; when he resigned, he was succeeded by Kerensky.

course, it goes without saying that he is not a great strategist, but, say what you may, his coming to take command of his army has been followed by a new, refreshed spirit. Who can say surely what is cause and what is effect? But the Czar came, and directly thereafter the tide of defeat turned. All over the empire a new hope sprang up, and Russia appeared to realize the presence of her own huge, awkward strength."[8]

And it was the Czar's own personal belief that he could give a spirit which not even the Grand Duke Nicholas could give, a belief which the Czar expressed over and over from the moment war was declared, which resulted in the Czar's taking command at the critical period when the Russians were being driven back.

The story was told to me by one of the ministers and confirmed by others who joined during the opening months of the war in begging the Czar to remain in Petrograd. The Emperor was told constantly that his presence in the capital was needed for the proper administration of the empire and because the bureaucracy feared that the Duma might take steps which would result in more confusion. He yielded. After the Warsaw campaign had begun, however, he asserted again his determination to go to the front with his army; this time he was firm. What followed was, in part, the result of the character of the Grand Duke Nicholas.

The grand duke is an imposing figure. He appears to have the height of two men, and on the top of his lean, angular whipcord body - there is a countenance of terrorizing power. The best opinion, gathered from those who have served with him, is that he is not in himself an immortal military genius; he is a great organizer and a great driver of men.

His figure and face appeal to the imagination of his soldiers; his organizing ability and disciplinary power to the imagination of his officers: he selects men for military operations somewhat as a president of a steel corporation selects efficient subordinates, and he disciplines with an iron hand assistants who are inclined by a national characteristic to be a little too fat and overfed, a little too complacent, and who, as a general of the Allies has expressed it, "are not rustlers." "He can break a chair over a desk with more dignity of anger than any other man I ever knew," said one of them.

It is impossible to find any evidence to support the more sensational stories that have been circulated about the grand duke's being sent to a new post at Tiflis in Caucasia. The commonest of these attributes his removal from the command of the army to fear that he would gain too great power, and might, with the army at his back, overthrow the present sovereignty. But this specter

---

8 Child is referring to the Brusilov Offensive of June 1916.

must have appeared, if at all, during the great Russian advance and before the metal strength of the Austro-Germans proved its absolute superiority to the man strength of Russia, and yet no move was made until the Russian people's faith in the invincible power of the grand duke had waned. Nor is it credible that at that time the importance of the present operations around the Caucasus could have been foreseen and that, as some have suggested, the grand duke was sent as a great strategist to cover the southern field of operations.

The simple truth is probably told by my informants: The Czar wanted to go to the army as its inspiration; the grand duke, overworked, nervous, having put all his energy into a masterful retreat, but appearing to the popular mind as a defeated man, was not pleased. He is said to have made the injudicious but characteristic remark that "the Russian battle front is not long enough for the Czar and myself." Whether or not this is to be believed, it is true that the issue was raised. And, that issue having been raised, the Russian sovereignty had no two courses to follow. The grand duke went, the Czar came, and, whether by coincidence or not, the whole tide of Russian spirit went from ebb toward flood.

Chapter 6

BUREAUCRACY AND NATIONAL SPIRIT

The Russian spirit when analyzed gives an answer to the second question, which takes the form of two questions: Will Russia make a separate peace, and is the German influence strong?

The Russian spirit is a little incoherent. To define it is difficult, just as it is difficult to define the power of Russia's sleeping resources. It is, like all things in Russia, a thing of contradiction. But Russia's spirit realizes Russia's resources, and Russia's own subconscious mind sees Russia more clearly than the outer world can see her. "For instance, when the Central Powers last fall drove Russia's army out of a vast territory the outer world felt that Russia had met a defeat which had shaken the Russian Empire," said Paul Miliukov to me.[1] "The empire was not shaken. There was depression. Losses had been great. But this war is not the Russo-Japanese War. The people in the last war were unmoved; the war was far away in Russia's back yard. This war is another affair; it is on the front porch."

The depression had a rebound; Russia's spirit surged back. And a part of its surging back is due to the fact that the Russian Empire is so great in extent, so rich in natural resources, and so well provided with endless hordes of men able to bear arms that it is like a great resilient lump. It may yield to pressure, as it yielded to Napoleon and as it yielded in 1915 to the Austro-German advance which swallowed Warsaw. But the lump retains its resiliency; it has a character of persistent expulsion. It may not be difficult to stick a thumb into Russia, but it is tiresome trying to keep it there. The lump is irritating with its resiliency. It is absurdly complacent!

For the outsider to believe that Russia must be depressed is natural. The financial situation is not pleasant. The ruble's value has slid down from about

---

1 Pavel Miliukov (1859–1943) was a historian by training who served in the Third and Fourth Dumas, hoping to find a legal path to create a democratic government in Russia. By 1917, however, he had lost faith in Nicholas II and his ministers and supported the creation of the Provisional Government. He opposed the Bolshevik takeover in October and eventually left Russia, spending the remainder of his life in France.

50 cents to less than 30 cents. No one sees any metal money. The Government printing presses turn out postage stamps to provide the country with small change; these stamps do not stick to the fingers, for there is no mucilage on their backs. The people have plenty of paper money which moves fast and depreciates somewhat less fast than the rise in prices, but the day of reckoning must come. What then? But there are the vast resources of Russia behind her credit.

Again, there is the fact of the Russian evacuation of her own territories and the destruction of the great army with which she started. But the territory is not a large slice of the huge empire, and there are almost endless resources of men. Russia is vast; Russia has a thick hide; she throws her great, incompetent, complacent weight back against the attack; she is persistent, resilient. She is a vexing foe.

And then the war has signaled to the somnolent spirit of Russia. It rises. It rubs its eyes. The struggle has made of the centers an extraordinary social congress of the empire. The war has brought a million temporary residents to Petrograd; it has increased the number of living beings in Moscow 50 per cent. Refugees, munition and relief workers, wives and relatives of soldiers who fight a night's journey distant, and of wounded soldiers and of dead soldiers have flocked into the cities. From all corners of the empire some of the subjects of the Czar of all the Russias have come together; back to all corners of the empire goes the awakening. It is not a surge of patriotism; it is a realization of that which we would call "new nationalism."

An American who has been in Moscow for four years said to me: "Could anyone feel this undercurrent of feeling - this terrible, elusive sense of Russian spirit - anywhere else in the world?" It is doubtful. And what is this spirit? Not our kind of patriotism. No; the Russian religion is in it too. The regular army was called the "Christ-loving army," but that professional army of more than two million is gone. And yesterday the regiment of newly-trained men from the inexhaustible supply stopped after drill to cross themselves before the cathedral. They believe that they and the inexhaustible hordes will not in vain fling themselves into a rain of shrapnel or a bath of lead.

There is even a sense of fealty in it: a curious, blind fealty to the Emperor, a fealty to a personified government which binds together this particular Russian human mass as perhaps no other than a modified autocracy at this moment could bind it. One man who from the peasantry came through university and "intelligenza" to fling himself against the autocracy has now hung a picture of the Emperor above his bed. "Internal reforms will come in good time," he says.

Finally, there is in it the reawakening of Russians to the sense of being Russian. It is the Slav consciousness. Next door, in Sweden, something of this half-concealed heart of Russia is felt; the type of Swede who is timid allows a look of terror to come into his blue eyes, and in these days he is speaking, probably without very good sense, of the Slav peril in a voice that more than justifies the italics.

The spirit marches with the army to the western fighting front and stands half in the shadow behind the more transitory enthusiasms of the privates. It is more complacent than emotional fervor and more persistent. And yet there is something fanatic in it, something Oriental, and it can breed fanatic self-sacrifice in the human mass.

A Japanese officer who with others is teaching the Russian artillery to use the guns sent from Japan was talking in Petrograd. Someone had asked him if there were truth in the story that guns made originally in Germany and used first by the Japanese to shoot at Russians were now being used by Russians to shoot at Germans. He smiled Orientally and, to divert attention from his failure to comment on a military secret, suggested that when all the facts are known the help which Japan is giving to Russia will astonish the world. "Not soldiers!" said a correspondent. "Oh, Russia needs no better soldiers," the Jap said. "Give a Russian a handful of rocks, and he will fight."

The X regiment of Russian infantry found itself on the outskirts of the town of Y. The men had been through a week of fighting; the ammunition supply had been cut off. And now, the depleted companies having struggled to a point where another attack might capture a German battery of field pieces, it was discovered that the whole regiment had only a handful of cartridges. The officers decided that a retreat was necessary, but the men took the matter into their own hands. With bayonets as their only means of offense, the regiment charged into the German fire, took the position, and captured the field pieces.

To make a separate peace on behalf of Russia is not now in the hands of the Government. "There could not be any valid negotiations, you know," said an Englishman whose function in Russia is to watch the progress of events. "Nobody talks of it, but even if something were signed in Petrograd, honestly I do not believe there would be any way to make the Russian army stop fighting. Petrograd could make peace only for Petrograd; Russia would keep on."[2]

As to the extent of the German influence in Russia much has been written. The presence of the German bugaboo some months ago made Russia

---

2 Child's prediction here proved to be far off the mark. After the Bolshevik Revolution in the fall of 1917, Lenin and the new Bolshevik government sought a separate peace. Signed in the spring of 1918, the Treaty of Brest Litovsk transferred huge amounts of territory from Russia to Germany, but allowed Lenin to protect and expand his hold on Russia.

hysterical. What is better material for gossip or the foreign correspondent than the spy story! In the German-conspiracy tale there is all the charm of romance, intrigue, and mystery. The detective story is a back number. And Russia succumbed for a time to the fears and the pleasures of the German spy and the German official-intrigue story. After the real tremor had passed through Russia, it passed out in the notebooks of correspondents seeking quick material. It had a rebirth in England. The *London Times* gave serious attention to the speech of M. Khvostov[3] in the Duma in which this ambitious member drew a terrible picture of the "German canker." The speech is now a matter for smiles among members of the bureaucracy, who refer to it as being a card played for the favor of the Czar and as having resulted in the appointment of M. Khvostov as Minister of the Interior.[4]

No one denies that German business interests had permeated Russia; much of the business management of the country and much of the Russian market had been allowed to fall into Germany's hand. Spies there were, and spies there are now. Even the German language had invaded Russia. Undoubtedly the Baltic provinces were filled with German names; German nobles and the German influence had reached the court circle and the departments of administration. Germans had made much headway in taking over the banking of the empire. They had tinkered with the tariff. But, to state it in a paradox, the German peril was small for the very reason that it was great. The German weed was well marked out in the Russian garden, and it was not difficult to pluck it out.

I remember a Cossack officer who talked to me intelligently about the condition of Russia. He was a lean, tall, dark-skinned fellow of uncertain age, who, with mustache and goatee, would have made an excellent Mephisto for the opera, but his cloak was not infernally red, and the hood of it was lined with spotless white satin, against which some gold braid glittered magnificently. The Cossack of a New York dream would have been a bearded centaur beating women and children with a knout held in a horny hand; this one was at a coiffeur's having his nails manicured. As the Englishmen

---

3 Alexei Khvostov (1872-1918) was a conservative politician and lawyer who held the position of Minister of Interior for five months, during which he opposed constitutional reforms and publicly accused Rasputin of spying for Germany. He had to resign after it was discovered that he had been plotting Rasputin's murder. He was executed by the Bolsheviks after the revolution.

4 For understandable reasons, there was much concern about German spies and other German influences in Russia. Later, it would be rumored that the Germans bankrolled the Bolsheviks, but modern scholarship has yet to prove such a connection and doubts its existence.

say, he was "a decent fellow and rather chatty." He spoke my language; he explained with some embarrassment that he had traveled three seasons with one of our Wild West shows.[5] Now, in more glorious days, he is an officer of a Cossack regiment: a regiment which, before going into a charge against the Germans, kneels on the ground and turns toward the east. He has been all over the empire from Caucasia to Siberia and across to Finland. "Who shall say that there are no families in Petrograd who do not in secret want peace with Germany!" he asked me. "But how are these individuals to act! If one shows his head, a noose is dropped over it. This morning the lady manager of my hotel was sent to Siberia; she had allowed German to be spoken in her establishment."

I stood with the editor of one of the great Russian daily newspapers. He waved his hand toward the street where the crowd on the Prospect were watching the afternoon war bulletins. Tan-clad soldiers with their arms in slings trying to salute officers in steel-gray, muzhiks and refugees in rags and greased boots begging others to inform them of the news, Government clerks with their portfolios, women, workmen, and one red splotch of the baggy trousers and the blue of the coat of a dilapidated French private who had come from Heaven knew where: this was the crowd, and there was something of the expectancy of the Russian nationalism in their upturned faces.

"Look at that mass, representative of Russia," said the journalist. "Can German influence touch it? Will it tolerate the idea of peace? And even then it is not the real Russia. The real Russia is the Russia which does not live in the cities. And it is awakened? All this is an answer to your questions."

In part it is also an answer to the rumors that come out of Russia that there is a possibility of a popular uprising. I remember that when I left the United States in October there were being printed stories of an uprising of the people in Moscow, of rioting in the streets, of an enforcement of martial law, of the clamor of unrest which was the prelude to a great upheaval.

What had happened was this: The Czar and the Premier, M. Goremykin, prorogued the Duma on September 16, 1915. The incompetence of the bureaucracy and the autocratic ministries had begun to enrage and irritate

---

5 In 1883, the famous American cowboy, William F. "Buffalo Bill" Cody, began a traveling "Wild West Show" that toured the United States and, eventually, abroad. Its acts included American Indians, horse-riding tricks, and sharp shooting, as well as Georgian horsemen who were advertised as Russian Cossacks. Buffalo Bill's connection to Russia began in 1872, however, when he and George Armstrong Custer led a buffalo hunt for Nicholas II's uncle, Grand Duke Alexis, during his three-month tour of the United States and Canada. See, Lee A. Farrow, *Alexis in America: A Grand Duke's Tour, 1871–1872* (Baton Rouge, LA: LSU Press, 2014).

even the bureaucracy itself. In Russia the great popular wish for a more complete constitutional government takes the form of a demand that the departments or ministries shall be responsible, not to the Czar, but to the representative national assembly - the "Congress" of Russia - the Duma. It was natural that, at a time when Russia was smarting because of the apparent inefficiency of the ministries and their bureaucratic machinery, this demand should be voiced most vigorously. The Duma itself engaged in a storm of protest against the Administration, and no doubt much of its criticism was justified. The criticism from the Duma resulted in two things: first, it spurred the bureaucracy to a higher standard of endeavor and stung it into a new state of ever-increasing fear of popular opinion and the latent power of the people; second, it began to create the semblance of internal discord in a country which, for the sake of strength in war, ought to have been acting in unison. The problem of the Czar was to decide whether these two results were too dangerous, first to the security of the bureaucratic system - which, good or bad, cannot be changed too suddenly - and second to the unity of national spirit. He decided in the affirmative, and prorogued the Duma.[6]

Those who are constitutionalists - and they are the people of Russia - were shocked and angered. Incipient protests sprang up everywhere. Municipalities sent petitions against this action, against which the Duma had stood as a body. Many members of the Duma went to Moscow and began to draw vigorous protests to present to the Czar. Public petitions were engrossed, and audiences with the Emperor were sought for the purpose of presenting them. The sovereign, however, was obdurate; in substance it is true that he would hear no one and receive nothing. Whereupon the representatives of the people faced a dilemma: the old, old dilemma of an autocracy resisting a demand for more complete constitutionalism and constitutionalists confronting the resistance of an autocracy. The dilemma was whether to try a test of strength or to yield. The Czar, having chosen the first, the Duma, the constitutionalists, and the people chose the second. There was not even the glimmer of revolution; I found in Moscow that there had been a street-railroad strike which, like many other Russian labor strikes, had its adulteration of political questions.

Paul Miliukov, leader of the Constitutional Democrats, or "Cadets," as his party is called, editor of the *Ryech*, said to me: "I am rated as a radical. But no one considers disruption of national unity at this time. The ideas of revolutions in Russia which Americans entertain often are absurd. Whatever the future years may bring to Russia, this is not the time for an uprising. And some of the leaders of my party have been criticized, when discussing radical

---

6 Explanation of Duma.

changes in the administration, for saying, as you would say in the United States, that we must not swap horses in the middle of the stream."

In Russia, the laborers, perhaps in a fool's paradise, are enjoying a temporary paper money prosperity; the civilians who have been hit by the war are refugees, scattered, homeless, and bent on self-preservation; the attention of the reserve army is centered upon the Austro-German battle front, and above all the empire is impressed with the necessity of internal cooperation. Not for years have the people received so many rebuffs from the autocratic machine, but not for years have they been so willing to bear all in silence. For enemies of Russia to rely upon disruption within is no more and no less sensible than it was for enemies of England to rely upon the troubles in Ulster to split Great Britain's unity.

On the other hand, the most serious menace to Russia is incompetence. In days when war is made by factories, and not by men, Russia is floundering. If the management of munitions and supplies had been left exclusively to the bureaucracy, a disaster of terrible proportions would have been visited upon the empire. If the day is to be saved, it will be saved by the cooperation of the Russian people. The organizations of the different local self-government councils into the war congress of zemstvos, the organization of councils of municipalities, and a commercial mobilization committee created only last fall, and called the Committee of War Industry and Munitions, of which Alexander Guchkov is president, not only aid directly but indirectly by forcing the bureaucracy toward efficiency. "The war has been in progress a year and a half," said the secretary of one of these sub-organizations to me, "but, unless it be on a steamer caught in the ice above Archangel, there is not an American shell in the whole of Russia." When I repeated this information to an official of the Government who has intimate knowledge of the commissions which have been in charge of procuring munitions, he scowled. "Who told you?" he asked. I was silent.

But in the bureaucrat's scowl there was the expression of a new realization of delinquency. It was an example of the many ways in which, by pressure from without, both at home and coming from the Allies, the bureaucracy finds itself driven to greater striving.

"We know that the situation has improved," said an officer who shared my compartment on the way back from the staff headquarters. "How much it has improved it is impossible for anyone to say. General Alexiev may know; General Hanbury-Williams, of the English army, attached to our Russian staff, may know. But correspondents must guess. Your guess is as good as any other."

My guess is that Russia is still having a hard time to provide weapons and missiles for her reserve strength in men. For this there are three reasons: graft, incompetence, and transportation difficulties. I have no doubt that I am contradicting a popular idea when I place graft last. Transportation comes first. The peculiar difficulties which make the Russian situation different from that of her allies are difficulties of ports and railroads.

Russia is a new and not an old country. Though the longest railroad in the world, the Trans-Siberian, runs from Petrograd to Vladivostock, more than 4,000 miles, and though there are over 100,000 miles of navigable waterways throughout the empire, there are fewer miles of railroad per square mile than in any other civilized country. The war has closed the empire's most used doors. If a manufacturer of munitions in the State of New York looks at a map to find the entry for his product into Russia, he will find Archangel reached by way of the Arctic Ocean and the White Sea, now frozen tight, and Vladivostock halfway around the world and still some 4,500 miles from the seat of war. A thin line of railroad comes south from Archangel to Moscow; a thin line of railroad comes westward from Vladivostock. The open gates are few and narrow; the way from them is long.

That there has been terrible congestion is no secret. No Russian official denies it, for it is known all over the world. Travelers across Siberia have seen the painful glut of freight choked down that narrow gullet of Russia. Archangel is a mountain of undigested freight. This vexed port has its wharves piled to towering heights with a helter-skelter of goods which just now is beginning to move. Fishing smacks in the pay of Germany sneaked into the harbor and planted floating mines. Among marine insurance adjusters in England it is well known that before this nuisance was stopped more than a dozen vessels were destroyed, and on top of all there is the Russian winter and its impeding snow. Archangel, from the position of a fishing harbor, has become one of the foremost ports in the world. More than a hundred warehouses have been built within a year, and yet while the water was still open an American steamer had to wait six weeks to unload!

To procure an open winter port at the north, the development of ports at Ekaterina, Kola, and Simons Island on the Murman coast of Lapland, has been undertaken. In the United States it has been said that American engineers are in charge of the completion of a railroad to reach 953 miles from the ice-free ports of the Arctic to Petrograd; in a modest manner this is denied by the Russians, who one finds are directing the work. The railroad traverses a good deal of wilderness; to Russia, however, it will mean much relief. How soon this route will be open cannot be accurately estimated. One of the greatest of Russia's weaknesses is the failure to keep promises; another is a habit of delay which would drive an American businessman to a sanatorium. I found that the road would not be opened for months after the estimated date, and that work had sometimes been pushed so far into the wilderness that the gangs of workmen had nearly starved to death through the failure to provide means to reach them with supplies. But every inquiry I made was met by suspicion, and any mention of the new road was discouraged.

To believe that this problem of munitions and supplies has been due to graft alone, as I have heard outside of Russia, is absurd. It is easy to drift in and out of Russia, finding how difficult it is to pick up facts and how easy to pick up rumors, and then go home to write readable stories of how rotten is the bureaucracy. It is easy for an American business representative coming into Russia looking for war orders to wander about in the catacomb climate of Petrograd, to sigh for "God's country," to wonder why the word Russia begins with one of the Cyrillic characters which has always been known in Chicago as P, and finally to give up and fall into the hands of one of the middlemen or "commissioners," who in bad English and a morning coat blame everything to "official graft." The war-order man, done to a turn, will at once claim that he was betrayed by high officials rather than admit that he was held up by an ex-barber. It is unpleasant to have to pay a "grease rate" for railroad and sleeping-car tickets; it is depressing to find that many minor Government officials want their "little percentage."

On the other hand, it is equally unpleasant to find foreign commercial representatives charging their expense accounts with payment of graft which was never paid, or to find foreign business men reciting stories of Russian graft which have no better foundation than that no one will require proof of them. In Petrograd, a fellow who had been trying to obtain permits to go to the front informed me that he had paid out over 200 rubles in tips before his passes were issued. I told him that I had obtained mine without any suggestion of tips. His expression changed. He said: "Well, I give in. I was fibbing. Tell me how you got yours."

I had heard that all petty officials would hold out their palms: I traveled about Russia, and was impressed by the fact that, with the pleasant smile of those who regard the foreigner as a guest, my offers, almost without exception, were refused by policemen, gendarmes, customs examiners, and soldiers. I bought a railroad ticket, and, wishing to resell it, I called one of the aged messenger "boys." I offered to give him all above 20 rubles which he could get for the ticket. He came back with 30 rubles, but would not take 10 of them. The old man stood before me, with his gray head bowed. The interpreter said: "He wishes you to know that two rubles suffice-more would be disproportionate to the service rendered and unfair to your generosity."

There is more of the heart than the pocketbook in the smiles of the Russian masses.

The drab blanket of sky in Petrograd; the retribution of anger expressed in the bells of Moscow; the sad, patient faces of streams of refugee peasants;

the great black blotches of ink and sand which the censor has slapped on to one's London newspapers; the white, bare, empty spaces in the midst of Russian dailies where news has been suppressed; the morning stroll of squads of legless soldiers; the faint odors of the Occident and the Orient mysteriously mingling - these are influences toward depression. But Russia, in spite of all, is not depressed. Russia is sensing a new nationalism.

The war has stuck a rude thumb into Russia's ribs; the pain will help to make a new Russia.

Chapter 7

RUSSIA'S BETTER HALF

The national character of the Russians of today and their social structure, both of which are in process of evolution, are reflected almost completely in the changes which are going on in one class.

The doctor of medicine and philosophy raised a pair of strong hands which had been used in surgery at one of the war hospitals in Moscow during the afternoon, and to accompany oratory at a meeting of the Constitutional Democrats - the Cadet Party - in the evening. "You will learn at last in America that this Great War will have its benefits," the Doctor said. "It is teaching us that we are strong; it has issued a call to us commanding us to learn to organize and act, not only in war but also in peace; it has taught us to see a world larger than the world of our family doorsteps. It has shown us that we can do all that is necessary to the old and true duties and, at our best, have energy and desire to accept new labors. The war has taught us! This morning at breakfast my children spoke of Russian victory. I said to them that the great Russian victories were in the new thought and visions of the people."

The Doctor did not speak of any class; the words were without any suggestion of distinction between different kinds of Russian hearts and Russian heads. There are almost twice as many men, women and children in the Empire than there are in our States; the Doctor seemed to include them all. The Doctor was nearing middle age but was still pretty, even in a severe woolen suit. She is an attractive and competent woman.

The reason for her unconsciousness of sex is not difficult to define. Russia is the foremost undeveloped country in the world. It is the Potentiality of our time. Like its own flat gray expanse of physical surface beneath which untouched treasures of resource lie, a crust of mystery covers the human resource of the Russian millions; the call and the charm of Russia is not in its romantic, hazardous, youthful past, nor in its picturesque customs of the present, but in the suppressed seethe of human force beneath the crust. What will burst up through it? What will this war, cracking open the surface, rending the cover, perforating the tegument, let loose? Surely far too great a human expansion to catalogue the sex of it. The Russian doctor spoke with a sense of values.

In lands where general development is abreast of the day it impossible to speak of a class which is behind. Our own women, conscious of lethargy or suppression, isolate their Woman's Movement. In Russia it is the Human Movement, and the women move with it; in Russia equal rights for women is a question not lost, but swallowed, in a yearning for rights for everybody.

I confess that when I went to Russia to put my ear where I could hear beneath the crust, the new bubble and heaving of the Potentiality, the volcanic seethe which the war has filled with new tremors, I did not think of the Russian woman at all.

She is of extraordinary importance.

Indeed her progress and her potentiality are so interwoven with the progress and potentiality of her country that the story of the woman parallels the story of the war-awakened Russian people.

More than this, it is the women, I think, who today are possessed of the calmest visions. From a woman I received the coolest and the wisest analysis of the politics of the Empire and the most sensible forecast of the struggle between the people and the bureaucracy. Through a woman I obtained the greatest fund of information about the future commercial development of the land, and about the opportunities for American business. A woman drew for me the clearest picture of what was needed to organize for military victories. It was the woman of Russia who without distortion of self-interest or prejudice or fear could see what the new human growth required of compromise with the present form of the government, and what of fight to the finish. And that is the most delicate question which Russia must determine in the decade which follows the war.

Three classes of women, just as three classes of men, may be distinguished, one from the other, for those persons who know little of the Empire.

Perhaps it cannot be reiterated too often that Russia is a land of peasants. The first thing one will be told in the capital is this: "Petrograd is not Russia. Russia is more than a hundred and twenty-five million peasants. My dear friend, about three-fourths of the people in the Empire live in rural communities or on isolated farms - three-fourths of us are engaged in agriculture, two-thirds of Russians are illiterate, and eighty-seven per cent of us peasant women cannot read or write. Ah! to know the true Russian one must go to the villages!" At last one desires to break the necks of those who drone so monotonous a choir of advice. None the less, they speak the truth.

To consider the Russian woman without due regard for the overwhelming numbers of peasant women, varying in types and customs according to the districts from which they come, is to exclude the mass. The nobility and small merchant class is the minority group of women; the proportion is about one hundred and thirty to one.

But even then all is not said, because among Russian women as among Russian men there is a third class characterized not by its exclusion from the other two classes which are classes of high birth or lack of it, or wealth, or lack of it, or position in governmental service, or lack of it, but by intellectual characteristics. Among women as among men this class is called the Intelligentsia, and an individual of it is called an intelligent.

"Define an intelligent," suggested a war correspondent from the United States who had a distaste for generalities.

The Englishman who writes articles upon Russian manners and customs slid down into his chair, the French diplomatic attaché scowled, an American who has done business in Kiev, Moscow, and Warsaw, for seven years, coughed, and the two Russians, one a journalist and the other a member of the Lower House of the Empire, the Duma, smiled sourly.

"What is meant is something which has escaped before it is captured," said the Petrograd editor, running his long forefinger about his collar as if seeking relief from asphyxiation. "An intelligent is an educated person - from a University - perhaps engaged in a profession - and perhaps with ideas of reform of Russia." "And yet there is Leonid H--!" said the Frenchman dreamily, looking across the tables at which well-gowned and smiling ladies, so different from the women of London and Paris, sat just as if war were not going on. "He never saw a University. His hobby was individual study. He is in no learned profession. He has no idea of reforming Russia. And he is a bureaucrat."

"But he, too, is an intelligent," the Englishman said, and the others nodded.

"Ah, there it is as always - an intelligent is an intelligent," the journalist cried out in despair.

The member of the Duma said, "Let us say that an intelligent is one who thinks."

"Who thinks--" repeated the Englishman, waiting for more.

"Who thinks and talks or writes of change," finished the Russian. "An intelligent is an intelligent."

"It will do," they all said.

The Russian Intelligentsia, however, has in its vague membership a startling proportion of women. The last two I heard conversing together were a Countess of immense wealth and the daughter of a peasant of the Tver district who speaks six languages and at the age of nineteen has published two pamphlets. It was two o'clock in the morning, and two professors in the University were present, but it was I, an American, who first felt that it was necessary to go. The zealous intelligent will sit up until dawn believing apparently that this, the latest discussion, may summon the destiny of the country; there is a taste for debate, an appetite for the last dregs at the bottom of the world's barrel of Intellectuality; and among all the eager Russian minds, most of which, as an incident, suffer from the inevitable pains of theories and pretenses which cannot be made realities by action, I found none so eager as those of Russian women.

The war has served to bring into higher light the character of the Russian people. Something of the veil behind which the Slav finds a complacent content has been torn aside by the emergencies of belligerent days. A titled English-woman pouring soup for the miserable refugee stream near the Warsaw station in Petrograd said to me, "You know by this time how baffling is Russia. It is a country of extremes."

"And contradictions," I replied. "I find I can say nothing about Russia unless qualify it."

"And yet – now - after years of living here, I think I see more of the human Russia than I ever saw before," she went on. "It is a great undeveloped force. It accepts life as life comes, saying over and over again, 'What does it matter?' but in meditation it builds a new world for itself. It flares up in emotional tests of its power and sinks back into philosophic lethargy. It is cheerful four-fifths of the time, and contemplates suicide for a contrast. It is conscious of autocratic suppression, but maintains the strongest kind of individualism. It is irreverent, but none the less religious feeling and religious forms grip the daily life of it. It is without conceit, admits its shortcomings with excellent good nature, and yet has profound faith in its own irresistible destiny. But there has been a great stir beneath the surface, particularly since the war. I have seen the growth of a new practical Russia. Will you believe that it is the women who have shown the potentiality to lead in this? The mystery of it is, how, with their history of suppression, they have in themselves so much capacity for calm efficiency."

Indeed this is a mystery. The past of Russia has invited the term "Barbaric Russia"; a much fairer adjective description is "Backward Russia." The position of women is a reasonably accurate barometer of the civilization of men and in the main the position of women until the last decade has been brutal; the peasant women have been like squaws - like the Iroquois squaws enjoying certain property and administration rights, and on the other hand the women of the upper class have been toys. To watch the revolt of both classes coming at one time, to see the quiet insurgence of both, which is based less on sex distinction than upon the general movement toward freedom for self-expression, to sense the beginning of a fulfillment of that promise of the Russian woman which has been held out for more than half a century by the succession of a few brilliant and noble representatives, is the reward of any one who in wartime observes Russia rocking toward an era of reconstruction.

I found a woman who had come from the peasantry, who could speak with authority about the standing of the peasant woman and who could look back upon her own early surroundings from the intelligence of one who has graduated from a university. There is, I believe, no other way for a foreigner to obtain a familiarity with peasant life. One modern Englishman has done it, but he has made a profession of the task. The other investigators of Russian rural life to whom I have talked can describe the village and its customs and bring back bits of handiwork and pretty examples of folk lore and peasant songs; they have seen the inside of the *isbas* or peasant homes, and the inside of the peasants' wooden bowl, but not the inside of the peasant. There are two reasons for this. In the first place, Russian authorities do not wish foreigners prowling about the villages giving out and getting in too much information, and in the second place the peasants themselves, as I found, are not lacking in a sense of humor or a sense of pride, or in reticence.

"I know an American who believes that he knows our peasants," said a Russian official who at one time was in Washington in the foreign service. "Well, I remember that once I was rushed through a mining settlement in a high-power motor car and I have thought ever since that I am an authority on life among miners."

The professional woman of middle age whose life had been spent in a peasant home, explained to me, as all Russians will explain, that there are further difficulties for the foreigners. Peasant life varies according to the districts, not only as between large divisions, as for instance, the Great Russians and the Little Russians, but even between village and village, and also changes constantly as the years go by.

The peasant woman of the past and present has been the victim of endless labor. She is expected to take care of the house, provide clothing and prepare all food. She often tills a plot of ground on her own account and labors in the planting and the harvest. At eight or ten the care of children is put upon young girls and from this time on, until a few years later, when they marry, the amount of drudgery increases. The peasant marriage is one often arranged by relatives for convenience and there still persist the customs left from the ancient tribal family, solidarity, community of property and supremacy of the ranking male which often causes the bride not only to be viewed as the property of the husband but as the property of his relatives. Moral standards vary from place to place; in some districts little chastity is expected, in others much. Many tragedies come about because after an association of love the young man is drafted for army service. Often when the moral standard for the unmarried is high, the standards for married persons are low. But it is always the woman who has the worst of it. Wife beating and other wrongs of a proprietary nature are not uncommon practices. In some districts, however, the women, in the absence of male representatives, are allowed a voice in the village council. Independent earnings are usually considered to belong to the woman; if she has labored in the fields of a landed proprietor the pitiful pay she draws is her own, and with the beginnings of industrial development the peasant women seeking larger independent earning power have pressed toward the factories to become more of the nature of persons, and less of the nature of property.

"Education has barely touched our peasant woman," said my friend, leaning over the wall of the River Neva, in a thoughtful mood. "Those who go away from the village to the cities and gymnasia? Ah, yes - but I refer to the education which comes to the country. And yet it is education which has already done something to help the position of the peasant woman. It is badly needed, for not only does it give the woman a sense of being more than a labor-animal, but it will raise her in the respect of men no matter how much they may clamor against educated women. Women who are labor-animals are much nearer emancipation than they would be if they were uncreative parasites. That is the strength of the woman of Russia I truly believe. Here is a bit of paper. I have gone to a bureau for these figures and you must show them to Americans."

She had taken her statistics from compilations made over ten years ago, but I could find no others of later date. I was suspected of seeking military secrets! The figures of the Russian census, however, showed that in rural economy and in industry and manufactures, more women were employed than men!

"You may be sure that education is needed by the peasant woman," she went on. "You see what a part she plays in our farm life, which is the life of the nation. Well, she as well as the man must be prepared to receive instructions in the modern methods of farming. We as a nation, with great resource in soil, and with all our tremendous production, are still primitive farmers."

I remembered that the average yield of wheat per acre in England and Germany was over twenty bushels, and in Russia less than eight! "And in the fight to live, too," she added, "Russia - particularly peasant Russia - has the highest death rate in the world and the infant mortality in the country districts is beyond your belief, and increasing in spite of all the work of the zemstvo doctors. Russia has a vast resource of healthy human beings, but she will lose it if she does not take care."

"The point, however, is this - the woman of Russia is quite different from the woman of America. I understand that in America a party of women seek to have a right to other occupations than motherhood! Ah, what a cruel jest to the women of Russia! The peasant women of Russia have almost an equality with men in productive labors! As long as this is labor of the hands and is done in detached communities, and there is no education, then the position of the women will be very bad. It will be bad for the sole reason that a female savage must accept all; primitively the distinction between right and wrong is settled by the fact that with the fist a man can strike harder than a woman. "Industry has been coming in and it makes a change. First of all, men go to the centers. But women follow and even displace the men. And children follow the women, too."

She had touched upon a great problem of Russia - that of underpaid female and child labor; cotton and hardware manufacturers had told me already something of the fearful competition of men, women and children for employment in industrial centers. Russia's industry has shown a marked tendency to centralize in a few industrial cities of mushroom growth, and around plants which employ great numbers of laborers. The peasants leave the country and the ancient communal idea of the agricultural class shows signs of fading away. At first the peasant, who is always land mad but whose holdings grow smaller because the population is increasing faster than acreage is acquired, plans to earn money to buy new fields - to go back to the country. But the drift is really in the other direction. The women follow the men toward the gregariousness of the cities. The war has augmented the movement toward these industrial and commercial centers, and it is these centers which are molding the new social life of Russia in spite of the fact that probably, even with the refugees and the congregating movement which the war has brought, not more than 16 per cent of the population is in them.

The factory wage earner is the new type of lower-class Russian woman and her influence spreads back into the agricultural class.

"For the moment we see some horrible things," I was told by a settlement worker. "We see the peasantry furnishing vast numbers of prostitutes, most of them very young. We see the great supply of female labor driving itself into starvation wages by its willingness to work in industries. But after all it is promising of a better position for women. They will find themselves. On the farm the woman has been too much a labor-animal. Once she or her relatives have a taste of the outer world there will be a new life of the intellect and a new and better relation between husband and wife. The independent earning of woman will tend to create new property laws fairer to women. The Slav woman will find herself. Put education within her reach and she responds in a way to give us all surprise."

To this settlement society, which like others in Petrograd exists by the donations and energy of advanced Russian women and in spite of the misgivings of some authorities, there come on Sundays hundreds of peasant girls who are now industrial workers. The contrast between their faces and those of girls in the villages is astonishing. The girl who has stayed on the soil has a happier expression but the film of an inactive mind often covers her countenance. These settlement visitors, whose clothes are so much uglier, and whose faces are so much harder, look without the rural shyness into one's eyes. They have tasted of thinking life. And this fact lifts their heads and perhaps their spirits out of the mire into which they may have put their feet. I do not believe that this new thinking life comes to them with any consciousness of sex-differences; women who for generations have shared in productive manual labor and now have not been behind the men of their class in finding a way through the muck of Russia's industrial growth toward larger expressions of self, look upon themselves as Russians and human beings before the idea occurs to them that they wear long hair and by its symbol are set apart in a class to fight with self-interest some kind of a class battle. I have seen evidence enough that when they are conscious of fighting a battle at all, they are only conscious of fighting the battle of all the people, men and women, for new freedom.

In the industrial communities the men, too, slide into the point of view which regards a woman first as a co-worker. She is capable of bearing children, but that is not against her; she is a co-worker. The whole drift is toward this recognition. Women are not only accepted as members of political parties, but they are accepted in the labor organizations, which, by the way, the Government prohibits, and are admitted to cooperative societies which sprang up to perform the "harmless" functions of the unions.

"The industrial labor class is our great menace," I was informed by a reactionary bureaucrat. "The rural peasantry is controllable. They do not seek innovations. But the working class is dangerous. It organizes for revolt. It furnishes the terrorists. It seeks to become intelligent. And the women you mention are in the forefront."

I confess that I found some sympathy with the bureaucratic fear of ultimate industrial revolt. The autocratic government of Russia is at least a government. At times it takes terrible, and often stupid, measures to suppress the people. A censorship, whether in war or peace, which aims to deceive, is a fact before the eyes of the awakening intelligence more irritating than those truths which the censorship can conceal. The fact that only half-truths go about in rumors leads to exaggerations. Secret police activities have stimulated rather than restrained the spirit of revolt. But were revolt to come successfully, the people of Russia could not today supply a government which would last. The intelligent class might set one up; but it would be too idealistic to be firm, and the unintelligent mass and mob would tear it down. It would be a Mexico raised to the nth power; and it is fortunate that the war and other influences have come to give the people a national spirit and a sense of restraint and in the end, a more deliberate manner of seeking reform.

"And yet even if the radical women are too eager for action, they must be credited with a large contribution of singleness of purpose," said a woman professor in one of the institutes. "I believe they wait with more art of restraint than the men. You must not forget the pain that comes to those men and women who acquire the education to see clearly, to think theories out, and then be utterly incapable of doing anything. This explains why reforms have appeared almost hysterical. I am an old woman, and I have seen the gloom and cynicism and the bitterness which have come to men of the Intelligentsia when reaction has surged back, sweeping the people off their feet because they were exhausted by their own protests. Nothing is so unwholesome as desire to put thoughts into action without ability to do so. This produces diseased minds and accounts for waves of suicide, and for the Russian trait which is named badly 'Oriental sullenness.'"

She had turned the subject from the uneducated Russian woman to the educated Russian woman. Unconsciously she had expressed her primary interest, which lay in the "intelligent" Russian woman, whether she be Countess or school mistress.

And after all, when one speaks of advanced Russian women one is speaking of that intelligent class; though it is numerically slight compared to the uneducated peasants, it is the significant class. Each new day of the many I spent in Russia added to my admiration for it.

The conception of Russian women to which so many Americans cling, reluctant to let it go, as if it were a sacred tradition, is that of sabled, cooing, powdered, lithe and languorous ladies who are irresistible, and invite from hearthside to suicide. Anyone who has seen Russian gentlemen in Moscow or Petrograd with opera glasses, lost in admiration for cabaret singers and dancers who would disgrace the management of a patent medicine show, could be convinced that the American notion of Russian beauty must be in some particulars faulty. There are women of too much weight - of body and of features - whom one sees about in the cities, and there is a large class of most refined and hospitable ladies who represent society, and whose many titles mean little because titles in Russia descend on the all-inclusive principle. It is nice to say, "I have just been at the Princess' to lunch," or, "The Countess dropped me a note," but it means little. One day a maid in a Russian home in which I was having tea announced that the Prince had come back from the front with a little wound, and was again at the door offering to buy rags. The ragman was, in fact, a prince - a Tartar prince.

Among the class of society women who include so many titled ladies, one who wishes to be gallant will mark the charm of their minds and the graciousness of their manner. Many are fascinating women whose minds are better trained and whose manners, though more direct, are more considerate and whole-hearted than those of our own "best people." But the "intelligent" woman in Russia looks without admiration upon the woman who is living as a respectable ornament. One of them, who has wealth and yet works eight hours a day in social service, spoke of the charming idlers as "the mewing women."

"I do have affection for some of them," she said. "But they mew so! This war is helping them to find out that they may stop mewing and do something. I have seen so many of the young daughters of their kind plunged into work in our hospitals for the wounded. I have two nieces who are going each day and really working. Ah, a good taste of usefulness will change them so that they will never be content to be dolls again. They will cease to mew. The flatness is truly leaving their faces."

The active, educated, self-expressive women of Russia who, from whatever cause, owe their stimulus to gymnasia, institute or university, do not have flat faces. Russian women are not pretty; many are ugly, but they have that beauty of active minds and excellent hearts which shines forth. The modem Russian woman has not much art in dress; there is little between the furbelows of those who pay much attention to styles and the dowdiness of the woman who is dowdy by nature, or merely too busy to pay attention to clothes, or too restricted in means. There is more modesty in Petrograd or Moscow than in New York or Chicago; in the Russian cities the adventuress imitates the woman of society, rather than the woman of society the adventuress.

To name the reason for the marked development of the "intelligent" class of Russian women is not easy. The answer of Russian men - even of those who do not approve fully of women who are not mere relaxationists - is education. This, of course, is the means by which the class is developed.

"Education has done it," I said to a young American girl who had come to Russia in wartime to study the Russian women.

"There must be something else," she answered. "The women of Russia have fought for their education for over sixty years. And more than that the Russian woman seeks her education for reasons in the main different from those of the American. So many of us go to schools and universities for a general idea of absorbing culture and preparing ourselves to make a good intellectual appearance. But today I have been at the Woman's College, and through one of the teachers I have talked to a great number of the students. It began to dawn upon me that in Russia most women seek education as means to actual service in life - as a pathway to real productive labor. They, just as ambitious Russian boys, have a desire to join in the actual fight for progress."

The impression that the Russian bureaucracy has opposed elementary education constantly is not correct. Scattered responsibility and clumsy plans and financial limitations have been the worst enemies of general and compulsory education. The population of Russia is widely scattered and to bring schools to all is nearly impossible. Furthermore, the schools maintained by the organization of the orthodox religion under the Holy Synod are suspected by the "intelligent" Russian of being seats of reaction, and the liberal teachers of the other schools, municipal and zemstvo, are suspected by conservatives of being the sources of radical and heretic doctrines. The zemstvos or local self-governments have done more practical work in extending the system of education than any other agency, and their schools, of which I am told there are more than 20,000, usually open to both boys and girls, give a four-year course. The municipal schools usually require a longer training. Toward these two classes of schools even the most reactionary supporters of the autocracy must take an indulgent attitude, because if an educational system is bound to be set up and no one dares to oppose it, then it is better for conservatism that the system be in charge of authorities, rather than existing by private cooperative management of the people.

Above the elementary schools which are beginning to lift the mass of Russian women from a wretched illiteracy, there are gymnasia and institutes. The latter are mainly for the daughters of landed gentry, bureaucrats, the nobility, and correspond, except in tuition fees, to our expensive boarding schools for girls of affluent families. The embers of the court have founded many such institutes and these institutes turn out the cultured, unproductively brilliant "mewing women." The gymnasia furnish opportunities for the girl not a member of the upper class who is striving to find a career of usefulness and ambition.

"But it is not into the higher education that the Russian woman has pushed her way," I was told by the secretary of one of the institutions for women on the Vassily Ostrov.[1] "There has been no marked resistance on the part of men as men. Keeping women out of institutions would appear to the average Russian intelligent as sensible as keeping out men with light hair and admitting those with dark complexions, or distinguishing between fat and thin persons. I believe we have less sense of sex difference than even you Americans, who are said to look upon women's desire to join you in an indulgent and good-natured way."

The college in which these words were spoken is a vast rectangular, gloomy structure filled with endless classrooms and laboratories. I noticed as the President took us about introducing us to both men and women professors

---

[1] Vasilievsky Ostrov (The Russian word for "island") is situated between the Large and Small Neva Rivers, at the historical center of St. Petersburg. From this island, one can see the Winter Palace (now the Hermitage) and many other significant historic buildings.

and instructors, that the curriculum had in it much of the exact sciences and little of history, sociology or political economy. The thumb of government authority had left its mark. But six thousand girls are enrolled in this one institution in Petrograd and there is in the direct, cheerful, active manner of these girls a promise which it would be hard to find among any other group of women in the world. Those students to whom I was introduced looked squarely into my eyes without self-consciousness, and though handshaking is much more of a custom in Russia than in the United States, there was something in the thrust and grip of these girls which spoke of better partnership between the sexes than yet has reached full development.

"The higher education for women began early in Russia," said the President. "You will hear of the young woman who in 1861 walked into a medical school lecture in one of the provinces and with note books opened, but without comment, took up the course. The faculty had never thought of such a situation, and there being no good reason to refuse, they admitted her. It was before that year that this college was founded with an endowment of not more than fifty English pounds."

From the middle of the last century the women of Russia have asserted their eagerness for the professions and professional training. Teaching, surgery and medicine and government service has attracted the greatest number. Where the medical schools were closed to them they went to Switzerland and other foreign countries. Nadine Souslov took a doctor's degree at Zurich in 1867. In the early '70's the admission of women to medical courses became a settled practice in Russia. In 1876 women surgeons in numbers distinguished themselves at the front in the Servian-Turkish War; the same distinguished service has been given by them in the Russo-Japanese War, and in the present conflict. Today women physicians are as prominent as men, and in some of the cities there are many more female than male dentists.

More than sixty-two per cent of the teachers in the zemstvo schools are women.

The census of 1897 showed that there were four women to every five men in the state and public services. In other professions there were more than four women to every three men.

I went to a Sunday night musicale at the home of a Petrograd merchant. The hostess has five children. The eldest daughter has left school to enter the relief work of the war; the wife has to manage the household and at present she is taking care of two refugees from Poland. She belongs to many organizations of women, but in spite of her many outside interests, her children, if one is tolerant of the unaffected self-assurance of Russian children, are attractive young persons, and her hospitality is of the constant, all hours, and informal kind.

"Will you have a cigarette?" a guest asked her.

"Oh, no," she said. "You will make these Americans believe that Russian women of refinement smoke. Furthermore, I have my work to do this evening. I shall have to be late to bed. And cigarettes are bad for one's efficiency."

I asked about her work.

"Oh, you do not know?" said the author. "Why, she is a distinguished mathematician. She has been engaged for several years in work the Government is doing - charting the northern seas and Arctic waters. She is a government hydrographer."

The women of Russia are not self-conscious concerning their abilities. If one expresses surprise at their work they express wonder at the surprise. "Why not?" they ask.

The Russian "Ladies' World," a monthly publication patterned after our own women's "fashion, fiction and fact" magazines, and other periodicals, are edited by women and women are often in charge of their business management as well.

One of my acquaintances in Petrograd was an active, diminutive widow whose son asked eternally and to my embarrassment questions concerning the fighting strength of the United States. His mother does not regard it as remarkable that she is a political reporter and an international correspondent, sending daily telegrams to a London publication about the fortunes of war on the Russian front. In her study she has covered the walls with military maps, and her bookshelves with manuals of military science, and it is impossible to convince her that there is anything extraordinary in her attempt to master strategy.

"I have a mind. It can grasp these things or it cannot," she says. "If it can - well and good. It will not be because I am a woman that it can. If it cannot it will not be because I am a woman that it cannot. And so--?" How often one hears that Anglo-Russian expression, "And so--?"

Women in Russia have not advanced to the degree that they do not foster women's organizations. No people are more fond of societies and associations than Russians. There are associations of arts, technical associations, musical clubs and endless societies. But efficiency in joint action is not yet a virtue of the Russians. They are too individualistic. The Government frowns upon any cooperative body which aims to do anything, and the Russians lack practice in acting together. Assembly is always dangerous, even when it is not clear that there is any political significance in it. Not many months ago members of the American and English colonies in Petrograd went out into the country for a picnic. The affair was conducted in a somewhat stately fashion, and proud men and elegant dames joined in the celebration. They were all put under arrest by the local police for conducting an unlawful assembly.

Russian women, however, have developed the skill to make their organizations effective. I went to typical "settlements" which are maintained by women's societies. Unlike our own settlements, they rely upon the cooperative labors of members more than upon their endowments. When the national relief committee under Prince Oldenberg[2] called upon sections of cities and upon towns for the establishment of hospitals, the "intelligent" women of Russia were in the forefront of the practical, business administration which makes the response of Russia so patriotic.

"The movement for woman suffrage in Russia occupies a peculiar position," I was told by one of the women reporters who had been attached to daily papers in Moscow and Petrograd. "You see, we have Finland near us and a tributary part of our Empire. There women have held full suffrage for years and years. It is a timber and industrial country and there women can not only vote but are elected to office and even assume political leadership. Finland has its own legislative assembly and a Russian governor, who at the moment is a man both unfeeling and unpopular. The women of Finland, however, have shown as much, if not more, restraint in dealing with the irritation of Russian interference, and the desire of many of the people for autonomy, than the men. We believe that Finland is loyal to Russia in this war and that Finnish, women are loyal. Then there are Sweden and Norway. Sweden, of course, is strongly bureaucratic because of the power of the governors of the different provinces, but in Norway the full effect of woman suffrage has been felt. Pray ask any Norwegian of the male sex about its result."

"And you?" I said.

"Well, we feel the influence," she replied. "There are many reasons why women in Russia would want to vote. They call upon us occasionally. When the first steps were taken against drunkenness long ago, before the war, and local option was tried, the women were allowed to vote because it served the purpose of the Imperial Council. But you must not forget that male suffrage in Russia is not even what it seems under our so-called constitutional rights. The first desire of the people-men and women-is for any extension of suffrage among the people. The question of woman suffrage is somewhat lost in that larger question."

---

2 Duke Alexander Oldenberg (1844-1932) was a medical doctor of German descent who had been born and raised in Russia. He was a member of the Russian royal family, a descendant of the Tsar Paul I's daughter. At the outbreak of the war, Nicholas II appointed him as supreme chief of the medical service of the military and naval forces. He and his wife were known for their philanthropy, funding the establishment of hospitals, orphanages, and schools.

Nonetheless, there are active suffrage societies. I am told that they are forbidden to maintain an existence, but under various guises they persist. The presiding officer of one of them in Petrograd talked freely enough about their work.

"We increase our membership list constantly and some prominent members of the Government who are considered reactionary would be surprised to find their wives and daughters secretly interested in our movement," said she. "Russian women are sent to attend international conferences of the suffrage movement abroad. We keep ourselves informed as to what other countries are doing. But we are very different from your women's suffrage societies. We spend much of our energy trying to show that women can be practical and efficient in government. For instance, I understand that in America if one goes to a woman suffrage society and says, 'We need better education. Therefore draw a bill for the assembly,' your women say, 'We do not understand education; if we did we would draw no bill. We bother with no political questions but woman suffrage!'"

I smiled.

"Well, how can they say so?" she exclaimed. "They must convince by showing in deeds how worthy they are in politics. They must seize all opportunities for political expression. How can anyone know their worth until they do so?" I declined to answer, and while she was showing me a copy of a new bill for compulsory education which a woman suffrage group had drawn for the new Duma, I reflected that the willingness of Russian women to demonstrate beliefs by practice was much of their strength.

When I left Petrograd for Mohilef in an army train, a young soldier who shared my compartment, on his way to the front, leaned out of the window saying good-bye to a young girl. An old artillery officer explained to me in French that they were married but that they had both been attending universities, and both expected to be doctors. The young Slav giant with his flaxen hair and clear skin roared with laughter, somewhat nervously, and the girl, tall, well-poised, rested her ample hands on the window-sill from without and chatted with a smiling countenance. They were Spartans.

The train started. The girl ran behind a post where he could not see her. I could see her bury her face in her elbow, shaking with emotion. The young blond giant turned to me and with tears in the corners of his eyes he gripped my knees and poured forth in a low thick voice a flood of Russian words.

"Ah! He desires to communicate to you," the old artillery officer said in French. "He desires to communicate to you that it is not difficult to say good-bye to an ordinary pretty woman to whom one is married and loves, but that it is much more difficult when she is also your best friend."

Perhaps there is in this a deserved tribute to the best of the better half of Russia.

The development of the Russian woman which, without question, is being aided by the war, parallels the development of the Russian people as a whole. The extraordinary human resource, the capacity of the individual to expand with training and education, the spirit of a race which struggles until it breaks its bonds, is now meeting the influx of the outer world with all the outer world's enlightenment of active problems. It will be difficult for artificial restraint to keep the Russian people in a state of being backward.

Chapter 8

THE MIRACLE MEASURE

The war has brought to Russia one change so beneficent, so extraordinary in effect, from which the results in a short space of time have been so marked and so cumulative, that not to observe and mention it apart would be to give it less emphasis than it deserves.

Russia has tried an experiment in nationwide prohibition; the impression it has made upon her social and economic structure is deep and permanent enough to make it impossible to say that of all the lessons of the war, from whatever corner of the conflict, any has a greater significance to the future of civilization.[1]

Upon the theory that the function of government is only to adjust the rights and obligations between man and man, and not to adjust the obligations of an individual to himself, and upon the theory that no restrictive measure is wise until a people are not only willing to legislate it but also substantially to live it, I went to Russia an opponent of any national prohibition. I promised myself to be an impartial observer, but I was filled with the expectation and perhaps the hope that I might take away support for my beliefs.

I was routed.

The facts overwhelmed me; I cannot see how a national liquor dealers' and manufacturers' league could go to Russia and bring back an adverse report on national prohibition. Russia has been an example of what alcohol can do to gag the voice of progress and make the colors run in the fabric of social organism - her national prohibition is an example of how the abolition of alcohol will set the tide of life running toward regeneration - over night!

In America on my return I found even sincere seekers of the truth who had succeeded in obtaining from Russia bits of evidence that the prohibition was being avoided, that the most significant effect was evasion of the law, that the law had made it impossible for those who had learned to depend upon alcohol to obtain it and hence many had died from deprivation or had tossed off cans

---

[1] Nicholas II imposed a ban on the sale of alcohol at the beginning of the war, hoping that it would benefit the public in general and, more importantly, those in the military.

of varnish or other stimulating poison in agony, and that the government itself was slyly breaking its own ukase.

I think these seekers of the truth succeed no better and no worse than will botanists who, wishing to prove that trefoil plants have no existence, go forth to bring back four-leaf clovers. The evasions of the law are so insignificant that they bear about the same relation to the observations of the law that the illegal entry of Orientals into our own country by the way of Portland, Maine, bears to the law excluding Chinese from the United States. The price of alcoholic beverages will always be the measure of the relation of demand and supply; when twenty-six rubles is the current price of a pint of vodka, prohibition may be considered effective.

True it is that, as I found, the abolition of alcohol in Russia has caused many deaths. If the prohibition were not effective, it is hard to see why these deaths have been so many, but waiving that consideration, the fact is that these deaths are not regarded from the same point of view in Russia as among the champions of freedom in our own country.

In Moscow the story is told of a conversation between a little girl and a kindly old gentleman who inquired why the crepe was hanging on her door.

"Father is dead," said the child. "Father could not get any vodka because the Czar has forbidden vodka to be sold. So father drank the fuel spirits from mother's stove, and now he is dead. God bless our dear Emperor!"

To the present time, prohibition against alcohol has been effective. Twenty-four hours spent anywhere in Russia would convince any child of ten or twelve of the fact, just as an equal time would convince any intelligent person that the results of the measures were miraculous and were making a new weave of the social and economic fabric.

"I am against prohibition," said an American correspondent to me. "But you will not catch me denying the efficiency of it here - not while I remain sober!"

Said a bureaucrat to me, "Evasion? Oh, yes, we have evasions of the law. Sometimes the evasion is of the law against alcohol, sometimes of the law against murder."

As for the Government, incompetent as it may be, floundering about with little cooperation between departments and with a bureaucratic system which causes each human unit to be a professional officeholder who is always tempted to hold his place first and think of Russia afterward, nonetheless it is the Russian which of all governments involved in the war has taken the bravest and the boldest step, and no one can come in contact with the Russian people without realizing that in administrative efficiency nothing can surpass the enforcement of an immediate and continuing prohibition over a vast territory and millions of people.

Today, looking back upon the closing of the government vodka monopoly, after one has wandered in and out of Moscow, Petrograd, and the Russian villages, and has taken the testimony of peasants, factory owners, and bankers, the complete enforcement of prohibition presents an inspiring retrospect.

One fact may never be driven into the intelligence of America: the Emperor planned the step long before the cloud of war had appeared; he said: "It is intolerable that the revenues of the empire should be raised at the expense of the economic and moral welfare of the people."

The actual beginning of prohibition during the army mobilization period was an order prohibiting all sale of intoxicants; it is still in force now. I have been unable to find a single respectable individual who wants to return to the sale of alcoholic beverages. In seven weeks among people and soldiers I saw only one pint of vodka. The people of Russia remember the disgraceful scenes which attended the drunken mobilization in the Russian-Japanese War; and today they all express astonishment at the effect upon soldier and citizen alike of abstinence.

The old peasant woman, bereft of husband, and giving her son at the front her prayers, has come in from the country to undertake housework in the city. To the little hut in which lived Peter the Great when Petrograd was building she has gone with other long lines of those who would light candles before the magic shrine. But she is canny. Her old eyes twinkled at the interpreter's question.

"Ah, good, good, good!" said she. "All the old topers are dead now. They could not get their holiday drunkenness. Alexis, the one-armed, tried to drink varnish. It killed him, and so much the better. They tell me all the hopeless drunkards are dead. The young people: they are not like the old either. They have been taught too much, and they are proud and wild as young horses. It is well that they should have no vodka. No drop of vodka should come back: no drop! All say it - young and old say it - except those who must have it or die, and these last have been buried already."

Across the River Neva, on the Ostrov, a factory manager said: "The Russian is not a steady drinker. He has been a holiday drinker. But when he drinks - oblivion! And in Russia we have an almost endless succession of holidays-holidays of state, holidays of church, and all 'legal,' as you call them. So it was that the average workman was on hand perhaps only four days a week. Now all is changed. Our men are here for all hours that the machinery runs. In so short a time have I seen wiped out infinite waste and misery."

Said a banker: "I thought the measure would have too grave consequences in its effect upon the finances of the empire. Do you know that the gross revenue from the Government's monopoly was nearly 30 per cent of the empire's ordinary revenues? Do you realize what it has meant to our war finances? But the step has resulted in the prosperity of the people. At the worst the money can be taken back by the Government in taxes, and even then the people themselves will be left in better health and with new productive ability."

The measure has been reflected with astonishing clearness already, not only in the productive efficiency of the people but also in their savings. The State savings bank in its statement of monthly deposits shows that the average monthly deposits during 1913 were a little over three million rubles; in the first seven months of 1914 the withdrawals were larger than the deposits. The prohibition measures came; then in the last five months of 1914 the average monthly deposits were over 23 million rubles and in the first seven months of 1915 the average was over 50 million rubles!

I am not an advocate: I am only reporting my observations. Today in Russia, to the credit of prohibition, there stands: -

An orderly mobilization.
A better trained and more efficient army. A reduction of crime and immorality.
A lessening of pauperism.
A general public opinion in favor of prohibition and its maintenance.
An increase of industrial efficiency which manufacturers and government investigators estimate at not less than 30 per cent.
A decrease in the economic waste involved in the consumption of alcohol.
A more certain resource for government revenue.
A new era in thrift.
A new generation of youth free from the alcoholic appetite.
Better babies.

On the side of alcohol I tried to find some one item of credit.

Great Britain had her opportunity to try the experiment at the moment the conflict began: her government lacked the grit. Russia had the courage.

Chapter 9

THE FUTURE OF RUSSIA

War may cause Russia to lose her best men in enormous numbers - already she has lost millions in soldiers and citizens – and the eugenic welfare of the empire, as of other empires, may suffer. Russia may lose ready-at-hand financial resources; Russia may lose a strip of territory which is enormous compared to Massachusetts but inconsiderable when compared to the area of which it was a part. Russia has lost much and may lose more.

But her gains will be great indeed. She will gain new national unity and new national ideals and new national associations with the outer world. In these Russia will have the opportunity to draw more benefit from the war than all her enemies and all her allies combined.

When regiment after regiment comes marching across the Field of Mars in the Russian capital, splendid men moving forward out of the winter mists with the swing, swing, swing of the Russian marching step, it is tempting to one's heart to beat in time with that swing, and for the breath of one's body to measure itself by the rhythm of the numbers. So the rhythm of the marching step and the unison of the singing express, I think, something of the new Russian spirit of national unity. When the Russian standing army was still in existence all this might have served to express the Army. But these men are reservists and men newly drafted; they express Russia.

These men could not express Russia if it were not for the war. They would not have been able to know so strong a national spirit. A year ago they could have expressed a certain Slav sense common to all, and each could have expressed the village, the canton, or the district from which he came; the national spirit, a year ago, had no such existence as it has today because a national spirit is spread very thinly in an empire where three-fourths of the people live peaceably and isolated in the country, where there are more than thirty acres for every living being, where the miles of railroad for each acre are fewer than in any other sovereignty, and where three persons out of every five cannot read or write. It is the war which knits the empire together.

The war knits the fabric of the national spirit by the bond of having a common enemy and a single cause. The process of this knitting is aided most by the fact that in war time the empire moves. Soldiers carrying the thread of national feeling go from place to place, from the country to the capitals, from the capitals to the front, and if still alive, wounded, dismissed, or on leave, return to their homes. Civilians, the women and children in great numbers, follow the movement to the cities, drawn by gregariousness in emergency, by relief work, by desire to be near hospitals where wounded lie, or near graves where dead are buried, or near trenches and battle lines where loved ones wait and fight. It is this shuttling back and forth which is weaving the new nationalism.

Feodor is a Russian soldier. A piece of German shrapnel entered his thigh. Therefore, discharged from the hospital, he returned to a peasant's home. This home is one of those wooden, heavily beamed houses with a thatched roof, yellow once with the sappy yellow of new cut fir, gray now with the eternal beat of the Russian winter. On the second floor, the dwelling floor of the family, where in cold weather the members sleep on the stove, are gathered the neighbors. Not only have they come to greet the hero, Feodor, but also to listen to all that he has to tell them; weak tea is sipped through tiny pieces of precious sugar held between the teeth. Thick but timid fingers touch the cross of honor pinned upon the rough tan frieze of Feodor's coat. There are silent old men who have learned so well two phrases in their long days: "*Zahftra*" - tomorrow; and the other phrase of fatalism: "What can be done about it?" There are the boys, belonging to an age of more education, who, unlike the old men, and most Americans, too, for that matter, have a realization that Russia is not an ancient country, but is even younger than the United States. They know that their country is possessed of limitless and untouched resources of soil and minerals, and that it is still waiting for an awakening. There are the women with their large working hands folded. All are intent because Feodor is the one person who in the memory of the community has gone forth to rub elbows with the whole of Russia - the whole of Russia brought together from the lands of the four winds. To them he has brought back more than his wound and his cross; he has brought back the empire.

He makes their hearts thrill by his descriptions of the endless columns of soldiers marching with the rhythm of the Russian marching step; he tells of the streets of Petrograd with their wide spaces; the sweeps of open snow upon the ice-locked Neva; of the strange funerals of the military dead, with the coffins carried in a grass hearse drawn by many black horses, each of which is attended by a man in a white duster and a white blocked hat and with a military band playing one of the awful minor-key dirges as it moves. Glancing at the ever-present framed icon hanging in its corner, he describes the chimes of the city cathedral in Moscow, the very sound of which, so terrible in tinkling of high-pitched bells, rolling up into the booming of hollow roars of a god in anger, is enough in itself to account for the eternal Russian prayer: "Lord, have pity!"

And perhaps this Feodor who cannot read nor write has gained more intelligence than the mass of the American people about the present administrative situation in Russia. He brings the new intelligence home. He interprets the Government.

The yellow and red palaces about the squares. and the river and canal banks of Petrograd are the seats of the country's administration. "Petrograd," says Feodor to the neighbors, "is a city of uniforms and functionaries." And the uniforms of the government clerks in these buildings of administration are a part of the uniform. display of many classes-the army and navy, the gordovoys, or policemen, the postmen, the boy scouts, the carriage drivers in padded blue kimonos with red belts, the liveries of the nobility, and the scarlet of court coachmen, the foster mothers, the students, the doormen with feathered headdress, the valets in red shirts and white aprons, the ancient and feeble "messenger boys," the dvorniks, who, as a part of the Russian surveyance system, are always on guard at the entrance of business buildings or dwellings. It is the uniformed government clerk and his department superior in a black morning coat who, under the Emperor, constitute the Administration. They are the bureaucracy, about which we hear so much. They are promoted from chin to chin, for a chin is a rank of service. They form a Russian class of professional officeholders who, like any other administrative functionaries, are sometimes efficient, and sometimes inefficient, sometimes broad of view and sometimes narrow, and occasionally dishonest. Altogether the machine is not satisfactory to intelligent Russians. The departments do not work together. Foreigners who deal with the bureaucratic machine find it irritating, for it moves slowly, decisions are hard to obtain, delays and broken promises are all too common. Feodor and the other Russians whom the war has shuttled about the empire carry home the idea that the country needs an awakening, that the bureaucracy must begin to allow the people a say-so, that out of peace, when it comes, there must rise a new Russia.

"This change of feeling began to be spread among the people during the Japanese War," said the editor of a Moscow weekly to me. "Knowledge of our own shortcomings was spread about. Dissatisfaction sprang from our inefficiency. What was the result! The result was the threat of a general strike and then the granting by the Czar of the form of a constitutional government and a supposed freedom for public discussion. The Duma proved to be only a step toward democracy and the device of putting cities and districts under special and so-called 'emergency' administration cut down the effect of political freedom and restored conditions in which for incautious political work or utterances a man or woman might be sent to Siberia. But it was war which then brought changes toward liberalism. Why? Because the war woke the people - because war started the truth traveling about the empire, from mouth to ear. That war was insignificant compared with this. At first we shall have reaction. You can see it going on now. But at last - at last - a new country!"

Already the interest of all Russians in other countries, and particularly in America, has grown keener. I came up through Russia in a railroad compartment to which the army authorities had assigned me on my return to Petrograd. Into my quarters I invited four petty officers of artillery who had no place to sleep. They were young university graduates from different quarters of Russia. One of them had been back eight times because of bullet wounds. They all believed that the United States is a country covered from border to border with Pittsburghs and office buildings. I astonished them as I astonished many Russians by telling them that three-fifths of our population lived in small villages or in the rural districts.

"In any case, we have rejected German management now," said one of them as the others nodded assent. "We do not know how to organize. We must learn. It will be organization - business organization - which will make the bureaucracy yield, and it will be organization which will build our tomorrow."

"There is something first - something before that," said another. "It is education!"

I asked if the war had emphasized this.

Of course it had, they said; everyone knew it. The army is not well officered except in spots, and the trouble is that educated men are scarce.

"I can't write orders for my gunners," said one. "It would be useless. They cannot read. So it goes."

They all stared at me incredulously when I said that almost every child in America could obtain an education.

"How can it be possible for the poor?" asked the second lieutenant. "I, like many other officers who have young wives, am sending my wife to a woman's college now. I went to school myself, too. I know that it is expensive."

"Elementary education in America is free," I said.

They did not disbelieve me. "The war is teaching us a great deal," the bullet-scarred fellow said with a sigh. "When it is over -- Well, the war is an education in itself. It is an alarm clock. It awakens us from slumber."

Until three in the morning they kept interrogating me about American education, American democracy, American efficiency. They were hungry for information.

"If you went to war, would your government be more competent than ours?" they asked.

I thought of the Spanish War and the bungling management of that tiny conflict in which our face was saved by the weakness of our opponents and a few heroic incidents for our schoolbook histories.

"Yes," said I with some doubts. "In this respect we would be more competent than you are - we can organize; we have had practice in acting together in peace, but Russians are unpracticed in organization. Germany has practiced organization in Russia. But Russians have not. It is Russia's greatest weakness."

There is almost no organization sense in Russia; the country has allowed financing and management to go out of its hands. The very word organization has meant to the autocracy and bureaucracy a rival force, and it is the instinct of the bureaucracy to frown on any group of Russians acting together for any purpose. Public meetings for any political reason are scrutinized, frowned upon, or forbidden. No one thinks of holding an open-air gathering except for song or picnic, or to bargain for and sell goods. The mere fact that A, B, and C acted together for any purpose whatsoever would be a danger signal to the secret police.

The day of Russian organization is at hand, and the Russian organization movements will be of two kinds.

The first is the organization which will come with industrial development. Russia must take up industrial development now, and industry is not like agriculture. It is a different fish to fry; the Russian Government will find it so. The natural limitations upon the organization of agriculture are many; industry, however, cannot live without organization. The growth of Russian industrial organization, now that Germany is ousted, will mean the existence of something new in the empire. Heretofore the reactionary government element could object to organization, but it cannot object to industrial organization; heretofore the liberal movement in Russia has been scattered about and has grouped and regrouped its demands and its programs so that there are endless and various philosophies of reform; parties in the Duma are split into factions; the people of Russia present no solid or constant opposition to the administration by the bureaucracy. But loathsome as the idea may be to many idealists and reformers - and I found it loathsome to Russians - willy-nilly there will develop a Russian business and industrial growth. This growth will have its organization, and this organization will have a clear, even if unpoetic, vision, and its demands for change will be constant. Business will know what it wants, and, will go after it. I heard the two Duma Socialists, Tehkheidze[1] and Kerensky,[2] address a meeting in favor of raising no issues of reform until the war was over.

---

1 Nikolai Chkeidze (1864-1926) was a leading figure in the right wing of the Menshevik party and served as a chairman of the Petrograd from February to August 1917. Georgian by birth, Chkeidze returned home after the revolution, but later fled to France when the Red Army invaded Georgia in 1921. He committed suicide in 1926.
2 Alexander Kerensky (1881–1970) was head of the Provisional Government from February to October 1917. He was born in Simbirsk and his father had been the schoolmaster where Lenin and his brother attended school. Kerensky was unable to stabilize

"And then - revolution," said another Socialist enthusiast.

No, not revolution unless I am mistaken, my friend. Cool heads in Russia believe the idea of revolution is ridiculous. Something less dramatic is in store for Russia. Business! That sordid thing - business. Clear of eye, persistent of purpose, capable of organizing a people back of its demands of common sense - it is Business which will be able to force liberalism on Russia. And it will do this not by revolution but by evolution.

The second movement for organization, if less significant in its promise, is more immediate in its effect. It has taken the first steps. It, too, owes its opportunity to the war, and is teaching the Russian people something of their own power. This second movement is created by the emergency of the war, by the necessity of help from the people to an administration needing help. It is the organization of war committees outside the bureaucracy.

There are three important movements of the people to organize Russia behind the battle lines - the union of zemstvos or of the local self-government councils of the districts, the union of municipalities, the commercial and manufacturers' union, the war and industries committee.

"The zemstvo has been an excellent institution for Russia," said a diplomatic attaché who goes with the Czar to the front. "You understand that over a large field now the zemstvo, though it may be in control of landed proprietors, is an institution of local self-government, and that it represents the peasants as well as the upper classes. Often it provides for villages and districts, government schools, hospitals, doctors, insurance and agricultural education. But this institution has taken on new life since the war began. From the central body representing these local governments has come great help to our armies-supplies, clothes, relief work, comfort for the trenches, bath trains, assistance to dependents who remain at home. The soldiers know it. The zemstvo institution, therefore, has new interest for the peasants, and those who are serving upon the committees of the union are realizing a new sense of organization and of real work. Talk has been supplanted by acts, argument by labor.".

A similar reawakening has been noticeable in the committees of the municipal government union. But unfortunately cooperation with these bodies by the bureaucratic government in Petrograd has been tardy and reluctant. Badly as the administration needed aid, it did not welcome with

---

the political situation in the months that followed the collapse of the monarchy, and was toppled himself by the October Revolution. Fleeing Russia, he eventually settled in Paris, where he resided until World War II, when he moved to New York.

whole-heartedness assistance which might serve to uncover the incompetence of bureaus, or tend to teach the people of Russia how to act together.

An example of the government attitude is found in the history of the Central Committee of War and Industry.[3] It was the conception of certain manufacturers in Russia that there ought to be an immediate mobilization of industries back of the war. Bogoslovsky and Kyshtym,[4] for instance, being metal makers from the Ural district and having large foundries and steel plants, came to Petrograd early in the war with proposals for industrial mobilization and offered the resources at their command. The Government wrapped their proposals in an envelope of official chill. Men like Chelnikov,[5] Mayor of Moscow; Riaboushinsky,[6] the head of the industrial mobilization work in Moscow; many prominent members of the Duma, Konovalov,[7] and even Alexander Guchkov, urged the necessity of enlisting the manufacturers of Russia. But it was not until the first year of the war had gone that the Central Committee finally was allowed to go to work.

Alexander Guchkov is considered by many Russians and many eminent men in England, France, and the United States as the ablest man in Russia. He was president of the third Duma and the Octobrist leader; he has the characteristics of a good business man combined with those of a good statesman. He fought in the Boer War, knows Balkan politics, and lost much of his prestige during the third Duma by attempting to work out a liberal and yet temperate program with the Premier, Stolypin. Some persons regard him as a greater man than Witte was. Guchkov allowed himself to be shunted into

---

3 The Central War Industry Committee determined the distribution of contracts, materials, and money obtained from the state, bringing together technicians, engineers, and managers, to coordinate production in various sectors including financial, transport, fuel, metallurgical, mechanical, chemical, labor supply and support services.
4 Boloslovsky and Kyshtym were both mining districts in the Ural mountains, producing iron ore and other important metals. Both would become extremely important during the push for heavy industrialization under Stalin.
5 Mikhail Chelnokov (1863-1936) was a Duma member from 1907-1917, first as a member of the Constitutional Democrat Party (Kadet Party) and then as a member of the Progressive Party. He was Mayor of Moscow from 1914-1917.
6 Pavel Ryabushinsky (1871-1924) was a member of an important industrial and trade family. He opened the first Russian automotive factory in Moscow in 1916. Politically, he was more liberal than many of his contemporaries, and helped to found the Progressive Party.
7 Alexander Konovalov (1875-1949) was one of Russia's biggest textile manufacturers and a member of the Progressive Party. After the abdication of Nicholas II in February 1917, he became Minister of Trade and Industry in the Provisional Government. He moved to France after the Bolshevik revolution.

the presidency of this Committee of War and Industry. His experience has been irritating.

"This irritation comes from two sources," said a member of the committee to me. "First, the Government has not helped us whole-heartedly. Needless to say, you will not quote me in connection with my name. Secondly, the truth of the matter is that Russian business men do not understand cooperation. You have said that the meeting which you have just seen had a more business-like appearance than anything you had seen since you left America. Alas, I felt it was only appearance. I have been in America and in England, and I know that the Russians are weak in the qualities which lead to organization. The Russian character is all individual, all independent; it is aloof, philosophic, and critical. When it is time to act together, we go and meditate separately. It is very sad."

I confess I took a more cheerful view. The commissions which have been sent abroad by this committee have shown efficiency; they have acted as a spur to the commissions of the Government.

Furthermore, the Central Committee has done an immense amount of work at home in Russia. Above all, any organization which the war has forced upon the business men and the local government bodies and the people of Russia represents the first step toward a country of new power, new vigor, and new ideals.

M. Sergius Oldenburg,[8] a member of the Imperial Council and secretary of the Academy of Sciences, is one of the keenest observers in the empire.

"Whatever may be the present adaptability of the Russians for effective organization, the hunger for organization is keen. The war is the opportunity," he said. "Scientific and technical societies, as well as the unions of local government and commercial bodies, have offered their services to the administration. Better and better is the reception given to these offers of assistance. As usual, representatives of the War Department or other government departments are assigned to sit on the volunteer committees. In many ways, therefore, the Government is learning of the unused resources of Russian public spirit, and our people are learning more of the shortcomings and the virtues of the bureaucracy. Our people are often called Oriental, but they have no Oriental characteristics; they have an undeveloped and gigantic power."

---

8 Sergei Oldenburg (1863-1934) was a specialist in Buddhist studies and a member of the Russian Academy of Sciences. In his political life, he was a member of the Kadet Party, a member of the State Council of Imperial Russia, and subsequently, served as Minister of Education in the Provisional Government.

The war has brought about another marked change, and this change promises to develop a new situation in the internal politics of Russia. The constant political struggle in Russia is between the autocracy, represented, on the one hand, by the administration of bureaucrats and the professional officeholders under the Czar, and the Russian ideals of democracy, represented, on the other hand, by the constitutional assembly called the Duma. The Duma came into being when the Russian desire for constitutional government was added to the dissatisfaction caused by the clumsy administration of the Japanese War in 1904 and 1905. It came into being because the autocracy feared the wrath of the people, and the marked limitations of its powers, because of the resistance of the bureaucracy, have been tolerated because of the people's fear of the autocracy. Thus Russia suffers from a steady undercurrent of internal conflict.

I talked with Professor Kovalievsky[9] of the University of Petrograd, authority on constitutional laws and forms, a member of the Council of the Empire and correspondent of the Institute of France. Old in years, still forceful and active in education and politics, a giant in stature, he is possessed of a rare characteristic--the ability to look down upon current history with the sense of humor and the indulgence of a good-natured Olympian. In the midst of the turbulence and distraction of Russian statesmanship, Kovalievsky sees the conflict go on as a grandfather in a chimney corner watches the contests of children. To him, I think, it appears plainly that the present issue between liberal Russia and reactionary Russia is whether the departments of administration shall continue to be responsible to the Czar or whether they are to be responsible to the Duma. It is as if our Congress was possessed of powers so pared down that its chief function was to furnish a debating ground and an opportunity for criticism of our administration; it is as if Congress should demand control of our cabinet and our departments.

But this is the issue only of the moment. The conflict is essentially a conflict between constitutionalism and autocracy.

"Each side fears to yield to the other," said Kovalievsky. "And each side fears not to yield."

I found that of the responsible foreigners who have lived in Russia it was those who had lived there longest who had most sympathy for the bureaucracy.

A commercial agent sent out semi-officially from England to study Russian economics said: "Russia is a thin film of people spread over vast territory and uneducated. This is a difficult country to govern. The bureaucracy is odious

---

9 Maxim Kovalyevsky (1851-1916) was a scholar of history, sociology, law, and ethnography, who was a member of the first Duma and the State Council.

to the democratic sense: it is most stupid, but the longer one watches the more one feels that any changes from the present administration must be gradual. And why? Because, in spite of the able leadership of some men, the Duma is not convincing. There is a great variety of divergent views and a wide range of beliefs and programs. Suppose the bureaucracy were wiped out tomorrow-could the constitutional assembly act with such harmony and sense as to give even a safe government to Russia? I doubt it. Personally, I believe it would mean utter confusion. That is why I, who am heart and soul in sympathy with democracy, am also in sympathy with the resistance of the Czar. If I were in his place I would fear that any disturbance of the adjustment might start an avalanche. You would be astonished to find how many bureaucrats are also constitutionalists. But constitutionalism must not be an avalanche, for it would bury Russia in chaos."

Paul Miliukov, leader of the Constitutional Democrats, did not share that opinion. "We would be confident in undertaking to build up a new administration tomorrow," said he. "The representatives of the people in the Duma have shown wonderful restraint. They have yielded, even in stresses, all other considerations to cooperate for the victory of Russia. It is the temporary efficiency of our empire which is fore- most, and the Duma and the people have shown themselves capable of foresight and wisdom."

But the effect of the war upon the autocracy has been to lead it or to frighten it into reactionary excesses. The autocracy finds that it can exercise an iron hand, and that the people of Russia make no effective protest. The Czar prorogued the Duma in September; he found reasons to postpone its reassembly in November; he refused to receive deputations of the people; he appointed M. Khvostov, a self-seeker with an unpleasant record, as Governor of Novgorod, as Minister of the Interior; the popular M. Krivosheyn,[10] Minister of Agriculture, he replaced by a reactionary, and he retained M. Goremykin, a reactionary figurehead, as Premier for months after everyone knew that Goremykin was scandalously incompetent. Goremykin was a tottering old man, so feeble and doddering that when he wished to rise upon the departure of visitors he often fell back into his chair and made so bad an impression that when I sought an interview with him I was almost told

---

10 Alexander Krivoshein (1857-1921) was a monarchist politician who served as Member of the State Council (1906), Assistant Minister of Finance (1906–1908) and Minister of Agriculture (1908-1915). He was one of several ministers dismissed for opposing Nicholas II's decision to take command of the Russian Army, but he remained loyal to the tsar and even joined the anti-Bolshevik White Army during the Civil War that followed the revolution.

outright the reasons for refusing me an introduction. But the Czar replaced him by M. Sturmer,[11] who represents also reaction in Russian development.

"As you Americans would say, the autocracy is trying itself," said a Petrograd banker to me.

There are, however, encouraging signs of a beneficent harvest of lessons which the war has caused to sprout in Russia. And these lessons are of two kinds. To the bureaucracy the war has shown terrifying pictures of its own delinquencies. Squarely, the bureaucracy was responsible for the retreat of the Russian army through Poland. It was responsible for the loss of Warsaw and for the loss of hundreds of thousands of an army unprovided with munitions and supplies. And to the bureaucracy the war has shown also something of the latent power of a people who await the opportunity to organize. To the people, on the other hand, the war has shown something of the futility of their disorganized, faction-split attempt to gain concessions for constitutionalism; it has shown the need and the pleasures of cooperative action as contrasted to individual brooding.

More than this, the war has brought out and is bringing out new political leadership. On the one hand, it has emphasized the value of a bureaucratic officer like Vice Admiral Grigorovitch,[12] the builder of the new Russian sea force and Secretary of the Navy, and, on the other hand, it has brought out the ability of such representatives of the people as M. Shingarev,[13] a Duma member of the Cadet party, who is head of the Committee on Munitions, and who has played such an important part in the work on the finances and the budget. Shingarev was a country doctor who entered politics with radical tendencies, but with a farseeing vision. Since the outbreak of the war he has won the respect of liberals and reactionaries. Conservative members of the bureaucracy have spoken to me of him with highest praise. The Czar conversed with him for the best part of an hour during the last Duma reception.

---

11 Boris Shtermer (1848-1917) was a Russian lawyer who held a number of regional government positions in various parts of the empire before joining the State Council and rising to the position of Prime Minister in 1916. His tenure is office was tainted with scandal, however, and lasted less than a year.
12 Ivan Grigorovich (1853-1930) was Russian noble who spent his life in the Navy, served in the State Council, and was Minister of the Navy from 1911 until the revolution.
13 Andrei I. Shingarev (1869–1918) was a member of the Kadet Party in the Duma and served as Minister of Agriculture, then Minister of Finance, under the Provisional Government. He was arrested by the Bolsheviks in late 1917 and imprisoned in the Peter Paul Fortress. He was later murdered by Bolshevik sailors in January 1918 after being transferred to a hospital due to illness.

It was Shingarev who saw clearly the necessity of a united nation during the period of the war, and he is one of the few men who have been able to counsel restraint, cooperation, and compromise without losing the confidence of the people who have learned to expect an eternal contest between their ideals and the forces of the Government. The war may cause this type of leadership, once tried by Alexander Guchkov almost at the cost of his political fortunes, to supplant the more impulsive and less constructive statesmanship which rests more on protest than on programs. The Duma has been much more of a body of opposition than a constitutional assembly; this the war may change.

"In a sentence, the war will exhibit the weaknesses of the autocratic machine and of the democratic machine," said an Octobrist member, "but remember that though the exhibit of weaknesses will tend to bring the two great contending forces together, there is always left more bare, more naked, more visible, whatever fundamental strength there is in each."

Just so. And a people who, in a great upheaval, have developed a national sense, acquired a knowledge of and an interest in public affairs, and learned that organized strength. is more powerful than disorganized unrestraint, are more fit to make demands. And a bureaucratic government which has been found delinquent, which fears for its own future and is tempted into arbitrary reaction, is weaker.

An autocracy which is securely intrenched can be indulgent and yield; one which trembles can be pressed to concessions. At the present moment in Russia the autocracy is in neither position and therefore is busy digging its trenches. It is a period of reaction. But in this very fact there is promise for democracy. The people will bear all while the war goes on; after the war reaction will appear to them more intolerable than ever, for the very reason that now the reactionary forces have tempted the wrath of the future needlessly and without foresight. In this fact and in the practice of restraints and organized power given to the people by the war lies the hope of liberalism and democracy in Russia.

But the war boons to the empire do not stop there; Russia is absorbing the ideals of the outer world, and the Slavic mass is changing its own ideals from within.

Chapter 10

RESOURCES AND DEVELOPMENT

The War of Europe is bringing us to a test of our international sense.

We must begin to apply international sense to our diplomacy; but we must also begin to apply it to our business.

We need just now all the international sense we can summon; we need it to grasp the extraordinary opportunities which the war will develop.

Of all these extraordinary opportunities to give the best of us, and receive value in return, none will be greater than that offered by Russia.

"But you Americans have no international sense," said a Scotchman in Petrograd to me. He has been sent out from England since the beginning of the war to make studies of future commercial opportunities in Russia, and he has worked so well his way into the confidence of official Russia that he is now an employee of the Russian Government in the work of collecting and arranging confidential economic statistics - almost a secret-service agent of Commerce.

He thrust his hands into his pockets and stared out the window at the regiments of soldiers drilling on the public square beneath the gray skies. He went on: "I wonder whether you Americans will ever develop that sense. You receive more immigrants than any other nation, but you know nothing of the hearts and souls of the lands from which they come. The English are stubborn enough in their self-satisfied content with their own manners and language and customs, but they are skilled inter- nationalists compared with you Yankees. And this is really your era. You can make more and better goods for the world markets - and for Russia - than any other nation in the world. Germany had the trade, but lost it. The rest of us are crippled. Russia will bound forward after this war. She is the one country needing development - almost a virgin field. But whatever you may be at home, in world salesmanship you are terrible duffers. Russia? My dear fellow, Russia is the Biggest Possibility in the World. But you won't see it. You Americans have no international intellect."

Have we?

The British have begun to see the vision of Russian resource. Officially and unofficially, England has set in motion new machinery to develop trade with her present ally. It is in the British and not in the American press and periodicals that one can find information in the English language about the new Russia. It is in London, and not in New York, that organizations such as the Chamber of Commerce have instituted Russian Sections. It is in the manufacturing centers of the British Isles, and not in Pittsburgh or other industrial cities of the United States, that manufacturers, even in the midst of war, have interested themselves in Russian export associations.

When I went through Norway and Sweden I met Danes who belonged to Russian societies in Copenhagen, going to Russia with something of the spirit in which men stampede toward a gold strike on the Yukon. At Moscow I learned that in France a government committee had been formed to work out with Russia plans for building new international trade. Riding across the Empire toward the Russian fighting line I met a group of Japanese. I thought at first they were artillery and ammunition experts going as others have gone, to help with the military problems; in fact they were merchants from Tokio studying the possibilities of the Russian market.

In Petrograd I found that almost every one could direct me to the Russo-British Chamber of Commerce which has had branches in Odessa and Warsaw; no one knew of the feeble Russian-American association. In London there are now at least five banks the titles of which contain the name of the Czar's empire or of its people. In Petrograd, Germany, England and France all have been represented by banking institutions based upon international trade and its credits. I saw nothing indicative of progress in international commerce bearing the brand of the United States.

In short I found in Russia that which any one with open eyes would find - a realization upon the part of all foreigners that the new, war-made Russia was to be the one biggest field of opportunity for investment and sales in the whole wide world. Do Americans know that Russia will rise from this war, a new Russia? Do they know that Russia, unlike any other country in Europe, is to be dependent upon foreign capital during her period of young growth, just as the United States in its young growth was dependent upon foreign capital?

Do they know that Russia is a continental space of territory, rich in oil, timber and minerals, crying out for development, and peopled by more than one hundred and seventy million, most of whom are white and yearning for progress, most of whom are capable of tireless work and most of whom today are misapplying their energies - the greatest undeveloped labor supply under the sun?

France, Germany, Austria, Italy, Spain, Portugal, England, are developed; it is only Russia which has remained in the cold storage of Europe.

Do the Americans back home know that Russia is the largest unopened mine of Future within the reach of finance and trade?

Alexander Guchkov, of whom I have spoken, is one of the big men of the Empire. Now he is the head of the Russian national committee which has charge of mobilizing industry and commerce for the purposes of the war. He has the quality of international sense.

"If someone could make Americans understand the new Russia, it would be a fine thing for Russia," said he.

There was something in his smile which suggested that he meant that it would be a fine thing for the United States.

Of course he was right. He is a Russian who knows Russia; and few Russians know it. Their perspective is blurred by politics, by war, by events, and movements going on too close to their own noses; and by a curious national characteristic of resistance to organized progress, their outlook is narrowed.

Russia needs American vision to see the irresistible economic forces and the inevitable social ends of Russia.

It is an agricultural country, the passion of it is land madness. Russia is a country of agrarian dreams.

More than once I have sat up into the small hours to hear Russians of the educated, reforming, meditative, argumentative type - the type which is called Intelligentsia - try to tell me what they would have Russia be. There was no fundamental difference of desire.

"Be concrete," said I. "Picture Russia as you would have her develop."

And it was a little woman in black, a journalist in Petrograd, and representative of the women of extraordinary ability who are now developing so fast in the empire, who, with her hands clasped over her knees and her eyes half shut, spoke, I believe, for the majority of Russians:

"I would not have Russia like the United States," she said defiantly. "We feel that your industrialism and your commercialism are repulsive. America is mad for dollars, for modern improvements, as you call them, and for luxuries that dollars will buy. No, Russia has a sweeter spirit than that to give the world: religious faith and a great love of mankind and sympathy. These flow not from the Government, but from the real Russia - the simple people.

"I would like to see that people remain as tillers of the soil," she went on, "but each - even each woman - would have a voice in government so that there might be freedom. I would want every person to have the comforts of good clothing, adequate shelter, and happy and beautiful surroundings, and - what shall I say? - the luxury of education. Ah, yes, the chief luxury would be education. Civilization, real civilization, is in the human heart and not in a vacuum bottle, or in your patent office, or the manufactures of Germany."

Truly, I believe, she spoke the Russian ideal - the Russian dream.

It will not come true. Wish it as we may, Russia after the war will not remain unsmirched by commercialism. It was Germany to whom Russia delegated the "sordid task" of industrial development. She allowed Germany to bring her metal civilization for sale to a people hitherto content with wood. The silver-plated fork is destined to supplant the wooden spoon. This is the fate of the world.

We know so little about Russia and that little we know is so distorted! We know about spies, and secret police, ballets, massacres, exiles to Siberia, the Jewish question, bureaucratic graft, and much of what we know is not so. We know a Yellow Russia. Most of our immigrants from Russia are not representative of Russia. They are not even Slavs, and three-fourths of Russia is Slav. They are not friendly to Russia, but nine-tenths of the real Russians, few of whom come here, are so friendly to Russia that they are willing to call it "Holy Russia" and believe it. More than that, most of the Americans who go to Russia and come back to report are not representative of the United States; they are adventurous journalists seeking to find the sensational mysterious Russia of the moving picture scenario, and adventurous commercial agents who cannot speak the Russian language, who are impatient because the Russian buyers cannot understand and because the middlemen to whom the business is so helplessly and foolishly entrusted, takes advantage of American inefficiency and of the lack of international sense and of our own unpreparedness in international trade.

First, we have not had the contact necessary to understanding.

Second, we have not today the machinery necessary to set up an efficient relationship with Russia.

I saw many times in Petrograd a roly poly Cossack, short of stature, who is beyond the age of military service, whose passion is economics, and who is never met when not carrying a book under his arm. It will be difficult to forget this eager man running along beside one in the mists of the Nevsky Prospect or crossing the snowy square between the Winter Palace and the red government buildings returning ever, again and again, to one sentence. He meant that sentence to stick, and it did. This was it:

"Forget all else, I beg you; remember only that Russia is food for the world, wood for the world, human power for the world - oh, this young sleeping giant!"

Russia is not the government of Russia, nor the cities of Russia, nor the Russia of the novels.

Russia is a world's timber supply. Of its eight and a half million of square miles, 39 per cent is in timber. Exclusive of Siberia, there are more than five million acres of forest, but including Siberia, the Russian Government itself owns over nine hundred million acres of woods.

Russia, developed, could feed the world. In 1915, while the war was in progress, the acreage in cultivation in European Russia was not diminished but increased; the Empire had over three hundred million acres in active agriculture. Generally speaking, modern methods of agriculture, extensive and intensive, are not in use. There is land enough; in the United States there are 30 persons for every square mile, but in Russia. there are only 18, and yet the population of Russia is almost twice that of the United States. In the United States almost half the people live in towns; in Russia less than 15 per cent live in towns. The people are on the soil and yet the soil in its extent and richness is almost untouched.

Under that soil are some of the richest mineral deposits in the globe. It is estimated that Russia owns coal deposits of more than 250,000,000,000 tons. She has copper to spare. The iron ore of the Empire scarcely has been touched.

And Russia is undeveloped. The story of the ways of communication tells this. A few weeks ago a group of Russian army engineers lingering at the mess table in staff headquarters were discussing with foreigners the difficulties which are besetting Russia in obtaining ammunition from the outer world now that the war had closed the entrances, except at Vladivostok on the Pacific and at the half-frozen water gates of Archangel on the Arctic Ocean.

"It is not only a military misfortune but an economic misfortune," said one. "Since the war began, our exports have been reduced to almost nothing. We owe more and more for imports and we cannot move our cereals and oils for exchange. But we see, too, how lame is our internal system of communication."

"Never have you spoken truer words," exclaimed the other, who in times of peace is engaged in the Imperial railway service. "We have about forty-seven thousand miles, but there is no country where shoes are worn which has so few miles for each one hundred thousand people. And there are 180 square miles of territory for every running mile of railroad, and nearly three-fourths belongs to the State and nearly three fourths has been built, within thirty years. That shows the youth of Russia, eh?"

When I repeated some of these facts to three American manufacturers, one of them said, "Yes, of course, of course. Russia is undeveloped. As you have pointed out, it is a land in which three-fourths of the people are farmers, three-fourths and more live out of towns, and a few years ago three-fourths could not read nor write.

"And as you say, Russia is a great plain sprinkled with picturesque and charming Slav peasants - a civilization of earth and wood and a good deal of warmth of human affection and all that sort of thing and very little progressiveness or purchasing power."

"And it occurs to me that Russia has been the same old backward boy for a long time," the other said. "And now comes this war. It kills off the male labor and limits production. It puts a staggering load of big debt and interest charge on the Government, it taxes the people, it creates a trade balance against Russia that is a nightmare and invites the country to slap on a high tariff in an attempt to bring that trade balance to normal. Why is Russia to be our Big Chance with a capital C?"

He can be answered. And this is the answer:

First, the war will not more than scratch the resources of Russia.

Secondly, the war has awakened Russia and it bids fair to make of that Empire a new nation.

In these two respects the position of Russia is unique among the belligerents. In developed countries the resources are not timber, soil, and unmined ore; in developed countries the resources are much more movable, spendable, destructible assets of wealth. In developed countries the human resource, the strength of the people, is only wasted by war; in developed countries, war has a blighting effect.

It is only in lands of great undeveloped human resource and undeveloped national character that, however war may destroy, it also sounds a call to action, growth, and progress. To be in Russia in contact with its bureaucracy, its people, its popular leaders, is to feel oneself in the presence of reconstruction and infinite promise. Today in Russia is a day of some efficiency and some gloom and some pessimism; but the complacency of Russia is for the first time disturbed, and complacency has been the great national fault of the Empire. The Tomorrow of Russia is a prospect which goes back and forth over the Empire like a whispered word.

Over and over again I have marked the new national spirit in Russia. It cannot be repeated too often: The war has made Russians feel Russian. Every day it brings movement to a motionless people. Out of the isolated villages come reservists going to the front, back they go to tell of Russia, and not only of the unrealized Russia, but of a Russia related to the outer world. The village mind thinks no longer in terms of zemstvo, or local self-government districts, but in terms of the Slav civilization and the Slav extent, and the Slav resource, and the Slav's relation to the nations.

In one of the small towns a little shopkeeper said to my interpreter, "The war has brought the world in to us. The Japanese War began it. Soldiers returned to talk. But now the mouths of the people are full of questions and answers. The world has come to us! If we had not had the war *you* would not be here. Is it true that Roosevelt is leading an army division into France? In America, do you care only for money? So we are told. But Russia is strong in many ways; you shall see it." ·

A Russian Red Cross nurse went down to Vitebsk on our troop train.

"I live in the Tver district," said she in French. "I went to the Woman's College in Petrograd and I have taught in our schools. Our people are sadly ignorant, but the war has sharpened their appetites for knowledge. Perhaps this will make a new Russia for us all. Education has been growing fast, but it has seemed so slow. After the war we may have it provided more and more until all Russia is educated. A single new generation may change wholly our present state."

In the United States one man is not distinguished from another by birth and title, but by ability and position won by merit. But in Russia there is a general unspoken recognition of the fact that it is accident which most often puts one individual into a class while the next man is in another. The result is a more fundamental democracy - a feeling of human equality and a strong sense of the sacred right of being a human creature, and being able to have affection for human creatures, of being able to feel in oneself and respect in others an individuality. The stream of good fellowship running between officers and men beneath all the extraordinary formalities of discipline in the Army is an excellent example; the reluctance of those in humble circumstances to do any homage voluntarily, or to be truckling in manner or bearing, is another.

"There is an accursed difficulty with this strong individualism," said one of Prince Oldenberg's assistants in the War Relief work, to me. "I see it every day. We Russians are so strongly individuals that we can't act together. The war is teaching us that we will have to do that. It is not sufficient to have human affection for each other and for Russia; we must learn cooperative human action. The ordinary Russian thirsts for it but hardly knows how to play a part in it."

No wonder! A people living outside of towns and in a land without industrial life must be unpracticed in organization. A bureaucracy, jealous or fearful of the power of people who have learned to act together, has for years frowned upon the words meeting, organization, society, association, cooperation, assembly.

"Lack of organization and practice in organization has shown itself everywhere," said a professor and Duma member. "In politics we know not how to combine for definite ends. We factionalize ourselves. We split and re-split."

That is Russia's weakness. It cannot be emphasized too often for those who would know Russia and do business with her.

"Team work, as you suggest, is not in their phrase book," I was told by an English journalist of long residence. "But you Americans believe the Russians are individually inefficient. Don't you believe it. A Russian will absorb more education in ten months than your colleges can pump into your boys in ten years. If there is any kind of work he can do alone he is efficient as sin. And when he begins to theorize about social matters he goes forward in leaps. I can't keep up with him - or her. But how to play the game with anyone else, he knows not. There are thousands of societies and associations and none of them *works*. There is no team play here."

But, mark it well, the war is effecting a wonderful lesson for Russian team play. Anyone can see it in relief work, in citizens' committees, in industrial organizations joined for munition and supply production.

I interviewed the secretary of one of the largest of these frock-coated committees, meeting in Petrograd. He pointed at the disordered directors' table which had just been deserted by forty Russian manufacturers impeded by the stupidity of co-workers attached to them by the Government's suspicious supervision, but most of all impeded by themselves.

"Oh, how hard they are trying!" he exclaimed.

Russia is trying hard. Probably nothing has ever equalled the war as an inspiration to try. It will teach more organization principle to the Russian people than twenty years of peace.

So it is that the war is an awakener of business Russia. It diffuses national spirit, opens the sluiceways of the Empire's social life to an irrigating flood of information which no censorship can stem, and teaches the polite art and the irresistible power of joint action.

This is the promise of Russia as a new opportunity for our trade and our friendship - not only has she the resources of matter and of mankind which she had yesterday, but a new economic development is bound to come from changes brought about, under the lash of war, in Russia's political and social fabric. This is the new Russia and we may well attend her.

Chapter 11

A CALL TO AMERICA

Russia is our opportunity. A prize is there not only in international trade but in a worthy international friendship. It will be a piece of national folly not to see this gain and not to strive for it. But make no mistake - the opportunity will not come to the door of the stupid, nor cry at nights beneath the windows of a people without capacity for international sense. Others will seek for Russian trade, Russian markets, Russian investment; the chance will not be served up to us sitting in an easy chair.

We must move. We must be up and at this thing. We must take those affirmative steps which fortunately are indicated clearly.

We must accept the view that mutual relationship, and particularly mutual trade relationship, requires, as any mutual benefit arrangement requires, concessions on both sides.

What must we require of our own government and of our own energy and commercial practice?

What must we require of Russia and of the change in her business manners and customs?

We need in Russia from now on, if we need it anywhere, a pungent diplomatic representative. The light of intelligence about the necessity of picking men of force with some visions of commercial possibilities and of affirmative, active international friendship in distinction to negative, passive, puttering international palaver, will soon dawn upon the American people. We need ambassadors everywhere with old-time steadiness but with their eyes on the future rather than reminiscent with memories of American politics. The ambassador's job should be one in which to see the prospect of a record, and not one in which to enjoy the retrospect of a record. After this war the United States will be dealing internationally as she has never dealt before. We will have no choice. We cannot stay out and we need to develop the international sense through the best and most vigorous men we can find. If present and former representatives measure up to that standard, neither they nor those who procured their appointment need worry; if they do not it will be a serious matter for Americans and no patriotic American will keep silent about visible delinquencies.

That is peculiarly applicable to Russia just now. Russia and the Russians misunderstand Americans.

"It is easy for Russians to conceive the United States as a country, smutted from one end to the other with factory smoke and with New York as the office at the front door," said a French attaché to me in Petrograd. "Idealism? Pah! They believe you are all money mad."

I told this man that when I was in Mogilev, at the headquarters of the General Staff of the Russian Army, the only touch of the United States I found was a Russian soldier who knew only four English words, - "Too proud to fight."

"Oh, they do not think that," said he politely, trying to reassure me. "They suspect not that Americans are too proud but that they are too busy and too sly."

None of the newspaper men attached to the Petrograd dailies with whom I came in contact would believe that the Ford expedition was not a forerunner of a systematic American commercial advertising campaign to be launched along with other misfortunes at the belligerent countries. And in spite of the fact that many Russians cling to the idea that the Peace of Portsmouth was forced upon Russia, I do not know how many said to me, "Roosevelt is different." It was a Russian banker who added, "There is one among you who rises above the dollar."

We need diplomatic and commercial representation in Russia of a standard of excellence which can eradicate a growing suspicion of our sordidness. While the idea of that sordidness and lack of idealism is suffered to remain in Russia there cannot be an international warmth. We need the proper official representation also because at the end of the war we must strive to make a commercial treaty with Russia. Our former treaty of 1832 lapsed in 1912 and the old tariffs continue to be applied "until rescinded."

"That will be a delicate matter," I was told by an assistant minister of one of the Departments of the Imperial Government. "What shall our policy be after the war? Who can say? The trade balance being against us will furnish an argument for a high tariff. We must restore our exchange. We must build up the value of the ruble. There is Longevoi, head of the commission for revising the tariff. Was it not he who spoke not long ago in favor of Russia developing from within; building up infant industries, keeping out everything which we can learn to make ourselves? And yet there is constant progress here in agricultural methods and so in production. The zemstvo organization is teaching new methods to the peasants. We can open our mines."

"And you will have new outlets," said I. "I understand that England has secretly conceded Constantinople to you in case -" He shrugged his shoulders.

"I was only about to say that our exports of cereals, oils, minerals, may soon restore us.

In that case a high tariff on manufactures would be thought by many to be a great piece of folly. But who can say?"

I asked how the tariff would treat German goods. I asked this early and late. The answer from sources of intelligence was always the same.

"The Government cannot distinguish against German goods after the war. Oh, we know that hasty English and Americans would have expected this. But the Government cannot, after a final peace is made, prolong the war by tariff any more than by cannon. No, no! Of course, Germany will lose her tariff favors. Many of us think that Germany tricked the Czar and his advisers in the Trade Treaty of 1894 and its revision in 1904. And of course there is no doubt that in the past there has been a strong German influence in the court and bureaucratic circles. It will never come back to its former power by which with a grip on our vitals, it exploited our country. German goods will return to our markets; indeed, German-made goods are still coming into Russia while the war is going on and by way of Sweden, so that the extra duties put on against enemy goods may be avoided. But the Russian people are filled with hate. Germans will have a different situation to face after the war, and the principal obstacle for them to overcome will be the anti-German prejudice of our people."

Germany before the war had about half the trade of Russia and a firm grip upon the sources of special privilege. She overreached herself. Her commercial invasion of Russia had begun to be the object of resentment of the Russian people. Between government and government it began to be plain that Germany was always seeking a little more than she gave. That the United States must not overreach is the first lesson we may draw from the German experience.

The second lesson is the lesson of German shrewdness and efficiency carried on outside the official channels. This lesson will be enough to show that all the trade treaties we can sign and all the commercial possibilities which Russia offers cannot by themselves bring to us the Russian market with its promising increase of purchasing power or the opportunity to invest in the impending development of Russia.

I have done what I could within a limited time to trace the story of the German trade invasion of Russia and I believe no man can stare down at the assembled facts without admiration. "There were necessary things to be done," a Russian consulting engineer who had his education in England and France said to me. "Well, Germany did them. That is the whole story. She was efficient and patient and you Americans will find you need patience. Our business men are not comfortable for your business men - they gaze into the smoke of their cigarettes and delay and dream. They will even sacrifice a little profit for a little complacency."

The Russians know that in business they are not wide awake. There is something primitive and Oriental in their trading. They even use a counting board with shining beads which we have seen in Chinese laundries. They like barter and drag it out to weary, unprofitable lengths. They pose. "Tomorrow," they say. "Tomorrow, tomorrow," as if they were above being hurried by vulgar business.

"Curse them!" cried out an American in Petrograd who is seeking war orders. "Even the styles in crowbars would change before these Russians grew tired of considering the sample."

Doing business with the Russian Government bureaus, just as doing any business in Russia, may be irritating to the American business man and at times will reach the point of blank absurdity; it is something to be overcome only by firmness and patience. Not long ago an American agent who had for sale a manufactured article for war purposes came to Petrograd, convinced that he could make a sale at once. He knew his goods were needed badly, and he was prepared to sell them without asking for an unjustifiable profit. With his letters of introduction he went to one of the bureaus; he received only an invitation to dinner. He was referred to other departments, and in them was offered many cigarettes and much tea. He discussed the war and national ideals. A week went by.

"Look here, the Russian way may be to engage in all this airy persiflage and delay," said he to the bureaucrat whose word would be final. "I will indulge in it if you wish, but the American way is to charge the cost of production and sales to the price of the goods. My time is worth now several hundred dollars a day. My expenses are large, and there are other charges to be made. Each day from now on I will add these charges to the price."

He went back to his hotel feeling that he had lost all chance of making his sale, but hoping against hope that by some good luck he would receive the order. Ten days later he announced to his friends that he had the contract; the price paid him by the Russian Government had increased at the rate of over $400 a day, since the day he delivered his ultimatum.

Not only does this slipshod, ancient and oriental attitude attach itself to Russian business men, sometimes in a ludicrous degree, but it is reflected in the Russian fairs which are just beginning to show signs of feebleness. I wanted to see one of the large fairs at which the flavor of the Eastern caravan still persists, and to some of which come traders from Khiva, Persia,

Afghanistan and the Caucasus. There are more than fifteen thousand annual fairs in Russia and the turnover is nearly $500,000,000. The turnovers at the two great fairs - at Nizhni Novgorod and Irbit - according to our commercial attaché, range from fifty thousand dollars to more than half a million. Furs, hides, glass, plated ware, cotton, enameled utensils, and formerly boots and shoes made in Poland are some of the goods bartered. I asked a young Russian attached to the Russian tariff commission why the fairs were losing their importance.

"Because Russia is beginning to learn how to deal in samples," he said!

This may indicate in some slight degree the amount of education in the manners and methods of modern trade which the American business man may expect to encounter, especially in the interior. It will be another call for patience, just as the petty graft, too much of which runs in the veins of Russian business, will be a draft upon the courage, persistence and patience of the American salesman.

A rascal of a middleman who is now vulturing American agents in Petrograd told me with a shrug of his shoulders, "Graft is not a Russian word. I think it was put in the American dictionary as a name for something you know first in America, eh? Ah, but what is the other
name - grease - well, grease is needed in Russian business and in official business. Not too much - a pinch, so! - a little grease!"

Even his manner had grease in it.

This is something for the American to meet and overcome. The average Russian business man and the average Russian official are honest. In the end with their help the American who has stood on a platform of honest goods and no graft will win. The two go together because it is often the attempt to sell dishonest goods or obtain a dishonest profit which gives the occasion for the payment of graft to the representative of the buyer. Integrity in trade custom is not set up in a day but it will come. "To be frank with you, the Jewish question will give you more trouble," said a merchant from Moscow. "I know that you will be displeased that I should mention this. But facts are facts and we do not like the Jew. If America is to do business with us she must recognize our prejudices. They are our own to do with as we please and we do not choose to deal with Jewish representatives. You will find, whether you like it or not, that this is a fact and a condition. You would not ask me today to deal with a Prussian in order to do business with you. You would recognize the sense of letting us choose at least a part of the conditions under which to establish pleasant relations, eh? You would not try to argue us out of our feeling? That would be a poor way to begin international friendship. Tell Americans then to be tolerant of our intolerance."

I have heard Russians who, avoiding politely the blunt words, said in substance, "It is quite all right for you to accept the Jews. You are not a nation; you are a boarding house. We are a nation; we are Slavs."

Some of the Russians, much in earnest and with great sincerity, have complained of our treatment of the negro.

These are matters in which perhaps Russia must in the end meet the outer world.

But in many ways the outer world must meet Russia and at once. I know of nothing more important to commercial relations with Russia than that our representatives sent to Russia should speak the language. It is only necessary to watch the man who cannot speak Russian thresh around amid perplexities and baffling mistakes and embarrassments and waste of time to be convinced of this.

"An office boy who could talk the jargon or even read the letters of the confounded alphabet would be a captain of commerce compared to me," said a president of an American corporation. "At least, he could call on a Russian official and find out whether he was in or out. Yesterday I went to find an iron manufacturer from Ural and after a half hour I found I was in the wrong apartment trying to talk business with a portrait painter."

But this is also the advice of all the Russian business men who are consulted. "There is much that is irritating in the Englishman's and the American's satisfaction with his own tongue," wrote one who was kind enough to answer my interrogations. "I know of case after case of letters and circulars in English flooding the wastebaskets of Russia. Even when a Russian knows a little English, and in these days of strife there are many of us who are learning, we have no time to practice reading on circulars and catalogues and price lists. I prefer Shakespeare myself. To be sure, German was made a commercial language in the cities; but to reach all of Russia and to make business worth doing, please write and talk Russian. Furthermore, as we have questions and want to tell what our requirements are, please send responsible representatives.[1]

"Turn the affair around, if you please. I have been in New York and I cannot imagine a store on Fifth Avenue ordering from Moscow Russian embroidery because a circular in Russian comes in the mail, but even if it

---

1 Though Americans became increasing aware and informed about Russia, its government and culture, in the last quarter of the nineteenth century, few people had the opportunity to learn to speak or read Russian until Isabel Hapgood, an educated Bostonian and enthusiastic Russophile pushed for the establishment of Russian studies programs at American universities; consequently, Harvard and the University of Chicago hired scholars with a focus on Russia in the 1890s.

were translated into English, would the shopkeeper be satisfied? Would not he want to talk and ask questions? Perhaps he will want to ask, 'Do these goods keep their color if washed? ' To write and ask - bah! That is six weeks wasted. So he would say, and it is no different with us."

The Germans had the sense to meet the Russians in these matters. They introduced the German language by being able to talk Russian. They sent out their mail in Russian. They had personal representatives in Russia; before the war, in one year as many as 50,000 Germans came into Russia on business. Some German business houses had twenty, forty, fifty men traveling about Russia in preliminary campaigns. It was the Germans who knew that a soap peddler who could talk Russian and had acquaintance with Russian character was a better salesman of goods, from cradles to tombstones, than the head of a sales department who could not talk and who did not know how to make a contract of any kind.

I had personal experience of American stupidity in Russian salesmanship. I wished to purchase in one of the cities a simple drug that is used as an eyewash. In several drugstores I sought to find an apothecary who could speak and read English, because I did not wish to take any chances of applying the wrong liquid to my eyes. In one of these pharmacies I found a line of drug products bearing the name of an American company, but the labels and catalogues were all in the Russian language. At last, in another small shop, I found a remote shelf of drugs of a second American company with the labels in English. Of course I was pleased, because this allowed me to find what I wanted; but a conversation with the apothecary conducted in words squeezed from three languages, together with a letter from the American house, brought out the fact that the line of drugs had been sent as samples several years ago.

The druggist laughed when he had managed to convey to my understanding the fact that he had never sold a single bottle. He was not favorably impressed with the idea of trying to sell drugs the labels of which no customer could read, and why he had kept these bottles he could not explain. The American company had written in their letter an elaborate apology for the labels and a more elaborate explanation of their plans to remedy the difficulty in case an order should be given. But the druggist could not read this letter and only understood its general contents; it was in English!

Another Russian merchant spoke of the American practice of quoting prices to merchants in the Russian interior F. O. B. in New York, or even at the factory, say in Ohio. How can a Russian merchant in Tver, who is just cutting his teeth in American-made goods, know anything of the processes and exporting companies and line of ships and rates and commissions and routes which lie between his store and the factory at Ashtabula. The Germans delivered the goods.

More than that, the Germans delivered the goods the Russians wanted! They did not make goods and take them over the Russian frontier and say, "Here is our product. Take it or leave it." That is much more the English and the American way. The German nation said, to the Russian, "Tell us what you want. We can make anything."

To that fact is due the hold Germany had on the Russian market. Americans, unused to detailed studies of foreign markets, will probably do what we are used to doing at home - try to create a demand for the particular thing we make. That is good. Business comes by this process of creating a demand; it will come in Russia as it comes anywhere, but the nation that will get this business is the nation which will find its toe-hold, not by telling Russians what they ought to have, but, at the beginning, asking them what they want.

In several peasants' barns in Russia I saw hanging iron-tooth rakes made with short handles. My American instinct would have been to bring long-handled rakes to these peasants and rely upon their good sense to see how many steps the long handles would save laborers. But when I looked more closely, I saw that the handles had been cut to make the rakes short. I came to the conclusion that the Russian had a reason. A man who came along with short-handled rakes upon which the price could be cut a little too, could walk away with the iron- tooth rake business for that district. Later on, if he invented a rake which would revolutionize raking, he would be in a position of advantage to create a demand for it. The example is a homely one but it illustrates a principle upon which our business men must act if they want the Russian market.

Finally, we must study the Russian banking and the Russian credit system.

"Briefly, this country is no checks and all paper," said my friend the Scotchman who is studying Russian economics for England's benefit. "The Russian of the cities uses banks for deposits but country-wide the old stocking, the mattress and the money belt are still in vogue. The checking system is not used as it is in other countries. Collections and payments are made by traveling agents. On the other hand, the credits of Russia are abnormal and renewals and discounts are the watchwords of the Russian system. Any nation which wants to do business with the Russians must meet the credit traditions of Russia. This means study of credits. The man who knows the credit of different Russian business houses and is willing to extend credit according to it being justified is miles ahead of a seller who wants cash because he doesn't know whom he can trust. It is a nuisance."

But the Germans accepted the nuisance and the Germans were capturing the business. Germans were planted in banks all over Russia to inform

German trading associations as to the credits of Russian merchants. Many German business houses preferred giving credit to taking cash because, if the credit was safe, the discount gave additional profit. Notes bearing interest at 5 per cent could often be taken to a German bank and discounted at 3 per cent. The way the Germans guarded against being caught by bankruptcy was to perfect organizations for the investigation and guarantee of credits.

One cannot long make inquiries in Russia without hearing the name of the famous Schimmelpfeng[2] in Berlin. His office was an inquiry office with branches in Russian cities and even at the Russian fairs; from Schimmelpfeng could be obtained the last word on the credit of the most obscure merchants in Russia. Before the war this bureau was being used by Russian banks and Russian sellers. Behold! the very seat of authority on Russian credits was not in Russia but in Berlin!

Germany did not only invade the Russian market with the patience and efficiency of its individual manufacturers and selling agencies but she did more - she *organized*, for the Russian business.

It is a lesson for Americans. Not only do we want an adequate official representation of our government possessed of some international commercial vision, but we will need sense in the campaign of our individual business houses. And yet something more is needed-it is the organization of the exporting interests of the United States.

A Russian-American Chamber of Commerce was formed not many weeks ago and has offices in New York at 60 Broadway. It is a beginning. If it succeeds in becoming representative of American business and does its work well it will plant active branches in Petrograd and Moscow and put in charge of these offices well-paid and vigorous men. They must be such men as will be able to build up without any subsidies even a better service than the Russo-British Chamber of Commerce now gives with the help of a small subsidy from the Russian Government.

I hope a way may be found for our federal Government to lend a hand to the work of having the United States known better in Russia. I would have those in authority find a way to name twenty or thirty Americans of such personality that they would represent adequately not only American business but also American ideals and would beg them to go to Russia in a body of at least a semi-official character. It would do wonders in making an international friendship, in creating a new understanding of Russia, and of us, in laying

---

2 Wilhelm Schimmelpfeng (1841-1913) was a German merchant who established a credit rating agency in Frankfurt soon after German Unification which would become a significant player in the development of modern international banking.

foundations for a new commercial treaty, in showing Russia what we have to sell that she has not the capital to make.

• •

Not to see the opportunity in Russia is to be blind willfully.
The war has awakened Russia.
She has infinite resource and deserves as a nation long credit.
She cannot manufacture all that she needs today.
Nor tomorrow.

Russia will have to make her own silver-plated forks or she will have to buy them from England or from us. The demand for silver-plated forks to supplant wooden spoons must come because so it is written in destiny, and Russia is a vast, undeveloped field of riches which from tilled fields and opened mines will produce that resource by which the civilization of silver-plated forks, vacuum bottles, patent towel racks, starched shirt fronts, and hideous electric-light fixtures may be purchased. If Russia does not purchase, she will be the first of all peoples to reject the terrible boons of progress.

Russia will not reject them. Way down in the center of Russia, searching for a telegraph station, I stopped in a village to spell out a sign painted on canvas in characters of the Russian alphabet. It said: "Potash and Perlmutter." It was the movies.

Russia may defeat Germany; it is civilization which will defeat Russia.

I regret it; perhaps Russia, in spite of all the nonsense that is believed of her cruelties and her barbaric heart, neither of which exists, is sweeter as she is.

But if anyone is to take silver-plated and patented civilization to Russia, it may as well be our own country - the United States. What will it cost? It will cost a tremendous effort. It will cost such an effort that Americans and some official Americans in Russia shake their heads woefully. But the prize is there. It may be a prize in the form of a new market, because if Russia decides to be an agricultural and raw-material country, she will take down the tariff and buy, buy, buy for 170,000,000 human beings. And if Russia decides to try to be a manufacturing country she will put up her tariff and borrow, borrow, borrow. In this case she will want American dollars and American brains.

Either goods, wares, and merchandise, or dollars and efficiency. We have both.

Russia will pay.

She will pay out of her forests, her mines, and her fields, out of the hands and brains of her great undeveloped human resource.

Perhaps most of all Russia will pay us by the contact we will gain from a people unspoiled, spontaneous in gladness, without hypocrisy, candid, complacent, whole-hearted. It will be good for us to be viewed from a natural philosophic height which mere education of an individual does not often attain; it will be good for us to learn to know those who see us as children, a bit dirty, romping with material things, with our toys of factories and steel rails and electric signs and chewing gum trusts, until we perspire. It will not hurt us to come in contact with a people who, as a people, suspect that our complicated material civilization is not only a failure, but perhaps an instrument of blight.

Just now we will meet a people reawakened by war and with a new capacity for recognizing the life of the spirit. If a new prophet is to arise with new messages for man it is probable that he will choose Russia rather than any point on the New York Central lines.

Knowing Russia will not only be good for the tired business man's profit; it will also be good for his soul.

THE END

INDEX

Addams, Jane 13
Alekseyev, Mikhail 25
Alexis, Grand Duke 7, 53n5

Black Hundreds 44
Brandeis, Louis D. 13
Bryan, William Jennings 12

Cavill, Edith 11
Cecil, Robert, Lord 11
Chelnokov, Mikhail 85
Chkeidze, Nikolai 83
Cody, William "Buffalo Bill" 53
Cossacks 19, 22, 26, 33, 53, 53n5

Duma 2, 3, 18, 31, 38, 42, 43, 46, 47, 49, 52, 53, 54, 61, 73, 81, 83, 85, 87, 88, 90, 97

Ford, Henry 13
France 15, 49n1, 83n1, 85, 85n7, 87, 92, 96

Gedroits, Vera Ignatievna 44
Germany 3n5, 4, 10, 11n2, 51, 51n2, 53, 64, 83, 91, 92; business acumen 10, 52, 105–7; efficiency 15; influence in Russia 52, 52n2, n3, 56, 94, 101, 106, 107
Goremykin, M. 53, 88
Grigorovich, Ivan 89
Guchkov, Alexander 46, 55, 85, 90, 93

Hard, William 13
House, Edward Mandell 12

Kalpashnikov, Andrei 25
Kerensky, Alexander 46n7, 83
Khvostov, Alexei 52, 88
Konovalov, Alexander 85

Kovalyevsky, Maxim 87
Krivoshein, Alexander 88

Miliukov, Pavel 49, 54, 88

Nicholas, Grand Duke 41, 42, 46–48
Nicholas II, Tsar: Children 43, 44; Peasants attitude toward 18, 20; Taking command of troops 47, 48

Oldenberg, Alexander 72, 97
Oldenburg, Sergei 86

Pau, Paul 15

Rasputin 2, 8, 45–46, 52n3
Red Cross 22, 24, 32, 37, 97
Root, Elihu 12
Russia: agriculture 93, 95; alcohol consumption 17, 75–78; backwardness 62, 74, 96; bribery or graft 55, 56; bureaucracy 87–88; chance of separate peace 51, 53; contradictions 41, 49, 50, 62; education 68–70, 82, 97; industry 83, 85; nationalism 79, 96; "orientalism" 16, 102; ports 56; possibility of democracy 91; possibility of revolution 84; procrastination and delays 56, 80, 81, 96; railroads 56; religion 14, 17, 28, 93; war committees 84–85; war refugees 29–40; women 59–74, 93; zemstvo 17, 84
Ryabushinsky, Pavel 85

Schimmelpfeng, Wilhelm 107
Shigarev, Andrei I. 89
Shtermer, Boris 89

www.ingramcontent.com/pod-product-compliance
Lightning Source LLC
Chambersburg PA
CBHW032029230426
43671CB00005B/256